EL Education

Core Practices

A Vision for Improving Schools

©2023 by EL Education. All rights reserved.

EL Education
247 West 35th St., 8th Floor
New York, NY 10001
212-239-4455

Design by Mike Kelly

Special thanks to the students of ANSER Charter School,
Genesee Community Charter School, Palouse Prairie Charter
School, Santa Fe School for the Arts & Sciences, and Venture
Academy, whose art work is featured throughout this book.

To view these and other examples of high-quality student work,
please visit modelsofexcellence.ELeducation.org.

Table of Contents

Foreword..V

Welcome to EL Education; How to Use this Book V

Design Principles..VI

Dimensions of Student Achievement...VII

Deeper Instruction Framework VIII

Character Framework IX

Attributes of High-Quality Student Work..X

The Five Core Practice Domains XI

Curriculum 1

Core Practice 1: Choosing, Adapting, and Enhancing Curricula 2

Core Practice 2: Mapping Knowledge, Skills, and Habits of Character 4

Core Practice 3: Supporting College and Career Readiness 6

Core Practice 4: Supporting Global Citizenship..8

Core Practice 5: Promoting Social, Emotional, and Physical Wellness 9

Core Practice 6: Designing Case Studies 11

Core Practice 7: Incorporating Fieldwork, Experts, and Service Learning 12

Core Practice 8: Designing Projects and Products 14

Core Practice 9: Designing Learning Expeditions 16

Instruction 21

Core Practice 10: Planning Effective Lessons 22

Core Practice 11: Delivering Effective Lessons 25

Core Practice 12: Planning for and Supporting High-Quality Student Work 27

Core Practice 13: Teaching Reading across the Disciplines 30

Core Practice 14: Teaching Writing across the Disciplines 33

Core Practice 15: Teaching Mathematics 36

Core Practice 16: Teaching Science 39

Core Practice 17: Teaching Social Studies 41

Core Practice 18: Teaching in and through the Arts 43

Core Practice 19: Differentiating Instruction 45

Core Practice 20: Teaching English Language Learners 47

Culture and Character 51

Core Practice 21: Creating a Community of Learning 52

Core Practice 22: Fostering Habits of Character 54

Core Practice 23: Building the Culture and Structure of Crew 56

Core Practice 24: Engaging Families and the Community in the Life of the School 59

Core Practice 25: Creating Beautiful Spaces That Promote Learning 61

Core Practice 26: Promoting Courage and Adventure 62

Student-Engaged Assessment 65

Core Practice 27: Cultivating a Culture of Engagement and Achievement 67

Core Practice 28: Crafting and Using Learning Targets 68

Core Practice 29: Checking for Understanding in Daily Instruction 70

Core Practice 30: Using Assessments to Boost Student Achievement 72

Core Practice 31: Communicating Student Achievement 74

Leadership 79

Core Practice 32: Fostering a Cohesive School Vision 80

Core Practice 33: Leading Evidence-Based Strategic Improvement 82

Core Practice 34: Cultivating a Positive Professional Culture 85

Core Practice 35: Promoting Shared Leadership 87

Core Practice 36: Leading Professional Learning 89

Core Practice 37: Ensuring High-Quality Instruction 91

Index 94

Foreword

Welcome to EL Education!

This book describes the full EL Education model. It addresses five domains of school that shape student achievement: Curriculum, Instruction, Culture & Character, Assessment, and Leadership. Along with our EL Education frameworks (presented on the following pages) the EL Education Core Practices provide our comprehensive vision for improving learning and bringing excellence and equity to all students.

This book represents more than 30 years of collaboration with school and district partners and scientific researchers to describe the ideal learning environment. It has been revised twice over this time based on our organization learning, current research, and on the practical wisdom and guidance of our partners. The structures and practices documented in this book are not simply aspirational: they are descriptions of the most effective practices in our partner schools and districts.

Within each of the five domains of school we have defined a set of Core Practices. The domains and Core Practices are not actually discrete—in the life of schools or districts, they overlap and boundaries among them are fluid. The domains are not sequenced here by importance or implementation order: all domains are important for student achievement and all must be a focus of continuous improvement.

How to Use This Book

This book may be used in a targeted way, focused only on specific practices, or it can be used comprehensively to guide a full expression of the EL Education model. For schools using a discrete set of EL Education resources, such as our literacy curriculum, this book provides specific guidance for the practices embedded in those resources, and also a vision of other practices that can be added to enhance student achievement. For schools using the full model, this book provides guidance for all aspects of teaching and learning and school culture.

For schools using the full model, EL Education conducts an annual Implementation Review to assess the integrity of implementation and its correlation to student achievement across all dimensions. Schools that demonstrate exemplary implementation and student impact across all three dimensions of achievement are eligible to receive the distinction of being an *EL Education Credentialed School.*

This book does not belong on a shelf. It belongs on your desk, marked up with ideas, questions, and inspirations. We encourage you to copy pages, post text on walls, and read excerpts in meetings. Customize the practices here to fit your classroom, school, and district. Use them to create school or district-specific tools for observation, reflection, and learning.

EL Education Design Principles

1. The Primacy of Self-Discovery

Learning happens best with emotion, challenge, and the requisite support. People discover their abilities, values, passions, and responsibilities in situations that offer adventure and the unexpected. In EL Education schools, students undertake tasks that require perseverance, fitness, craftsmanship, imagination, self-discipline, and significant achievement. A teacher's primary task is to help students overcome their fears and discover they can do more than they think they can.

2. The Having of Wonderful Ideas

Teaching in EL Education schools fosters curiosity about the world by creating learning situations that provide something important to think about, time to experiment, and time to make sense of what is observed.

3. The Responsibility for Learning

Learning is both a personal process of discovery and a social activity. Everyone learns both individually and as part of a group. Every aspect of an EL Education school encourages both children and adults to become increasingly responsible for directing their own personal and collective learning.

4. Empathy and Caring

Learning is fostered best in communities where students' and teachers' ideas are respected and where there is mutual trust. Learning groups are small in EL Education schools, with a caring adult looking after the progress and acting as an advocate for each child. Older students mentor younger ones, and students feel physically and emotionally safe.

5. Success and Failure

All students need to be successful if they are to build the confidence and capacity to take risks and meet increasingly difficult challenges. But it is also important for students to learn from their failures, to persevere when things are hard, and to learn to turn disabilities into opportunities.

6. Collaboration and Competition

Individual development and group development are integrated so that the value of friendship, trust, and group action is clear. Students are encouraged to compete, not against each other, but with their own personal best and with rigorous standards of excellence.

7. Diversity and Inclusion

Both diversity and inclusion increase the richness of ideas, creative power, problem-solving ability, and respect for others. In EL Education schools, students investigate and value their different histories and talents as well as those of other communities and cultures. Schools and learning groups are heterogeneous.

8. The Natural World

A direct and respectful relationship with the natural world refreshes the human spirit and teaches the important ideas of recurring cycles and cause and effect. Students learn to become stewards of the earth and of future generations.

9. Solitude and Reflection

Students and teachers need time alone to explore their own thoughts, make their own connections, and create their own ideas. They also need to exchange their reflections with other students and with adults.

10. Service and Compassion

We are crew, not passengers. Students and teachers are strengthened by acts of consequential service to others, and one of an EL Education school's primary functions is to prepare students with the attitudes and skills to learn from and be of service.

EL Education Dimensions of Student Achievement

Our definition of student achievement combines academic achievement, character, and high-quality work. We believe that academic success is built on strong character qualities of collaboration, perseverance, responsibility, and compassion, and that character is shaped through engaging and challenging academic work.

Dimension of Achievement	Students	Teachers and Leaders
Mastery of Knowledge and Skills	• **Demonstrate proficiency and deeper understanding:** show mastery in a body of knowledge and skills within each discipline • **Apply their learning:** transfer knowledge and skills to novel, meaningful tasks • **Think critically:** analyze, evaluate, and synthesize complex ideas and consider multiple perspectives • **Communicate clearly:** write, speak, and present ideas effectively in a variety of media within and across disciplines	• Ensure that curriculum, instruction, and assessments are **rigorous, meaningful, and aligned with standards** • **Use assessment practices** that position students as leaders of their own learning • Use **meaningful data for both teachers and students to track progress** toward learning goals • **Engage all students in daily lessons that require critical thinking** about complex, worthy ideas, texts, and problems
Character	• **Work to become effective learners:** develop the mindsets and skills for success in college, career, and life (e.g., initiative, responsibility, perseverance, collaboration) • **Work to become ethical people:** treat others well and stand up for what is right (e.g., empathy, integrity, respect, compassion) • **Contribute to a better world:** put their learning to use to improve communities (e.g., citizenship, service)	• **Elevate student voice and leadership** in classrooms and across the school • **Make habits of scholarship visible** across the school and in daily instruction • Model a **school-wide culture of respect and compassion** • **Prioritize social and emotional learning,** along with academic learning, across the school
High-Quality Student Work	• **Create complex work:** demonstrate higher-order thinking, multiple perspectives and transfer of understanding • **Demonstrate craftsmanship:** create work that is accurate and beautiful in conception and execution • **Create authentic work:** demonstrate original thinking and voice, connect to real-world issues and formats, and when possible, create work that is meaningful to the community beyond the school	• **Design tasks that ask students to apply, analyze, evaluate and create** as part of their work • **Use models of excellence, critique, and multiple drafts** to support all students to produce work of exceptional quality • **Connect students to the world beyond school** through meaningful fieldwork, expert collaborators, research, and service learning

Deeper Instruction Framework

Challenging

Learning is courageous; it embraces a process of risk taking, growth, and revision.

- Students may struggle individually and collectively; they expect to make mistakes along the way.
- Students understand that uncertainty, grappling, and/or playful exploration are a part of learning.
- Teachers explicitly and implicitly communicate a growth mindset to students.

Learning is planned to meet and exceed standards.

- Students are working at tasks and toward targets that are clearly aligned with standards and, when possible, go beyond standards.
- Students demonstrate understanding of disciplinary big ideas, ways of thinking, and skills.
- Students apply their understanding to produce work that demonstrates complexity, craftsmanship, and authenticity.

Learning is cognitively rigorous.

- Students are applying, analyzing, evaluating, and/or creating during a significant portion of the lesson or arc of lessons (not simply remembering).
- Students think critically. They synthesize complex ideas and consider multiple perspectives.

Engaging

Learning is active.

- Students are engaged in productive work throughout the class.
- Students create ideas and work that have value and are worthy of peer and class discussion and critique.
- Teachers regularly use protocols and strategies that encourage all students to participate and be accountable for learning.

Learning results from pursuing worthy questions.

- Teachers and students ask questions that promote critical thinking and inquiry.
- Students are given sustained opportunities to ask questions and engage in scholarly dialogue with other students.
- Students ask and answer questions that require reading, writing, and using evidence from sources, or require mathematical and scientific exploration.

Learning is purposeful.

- Students understand how their new learning connects to past learning (i.e., not a series of disconnected lessons).
- Students understand how the work they are doing connects to real-world issues, needs, careers, and lives.
- When appropriate, students do work that simulates professional work that happens in the discipline or field.

Empowering

Learning fosters responsibility.

- Students become ethical people and effective learners who develop the mindsets, skills, and character they need for success in college, career, and life.
- Students have specific roles and responsibilities for working in groups and learn to collaborate and communicate effectively.
- Students put their learning to use to improve their communities.
- Teachers elevate student voice and leadership in classrooms and across the school.

Learning is self-assessed and peer-assessed.

- Teachers involve students in discussing and creating goals for learning and criteria for success.
- Teachers provide frequent feedback to students along the way and teach students how to self-assess, revise, and critique and support peers.
- Students reflect on and track their own progress toward learning targets based on meaningful data.
- Students have regular opportunities to debrief learning experiences.

Learning inspires students to create work of high quality.

- Teachers have high expectations and provide thoughtful scaffolding to support high-quality work.
- Students use models, critique, and descriptive feedback to improve their work through multiple drafts.
- Students create work that is of higher quality than they thought was possible and take pride in their own craftsmanship and growth.
- Students can articulate why their learning matters and transfer knowledge and skills to novel, meaningful tasks and situations.

EL Education
Character Framework

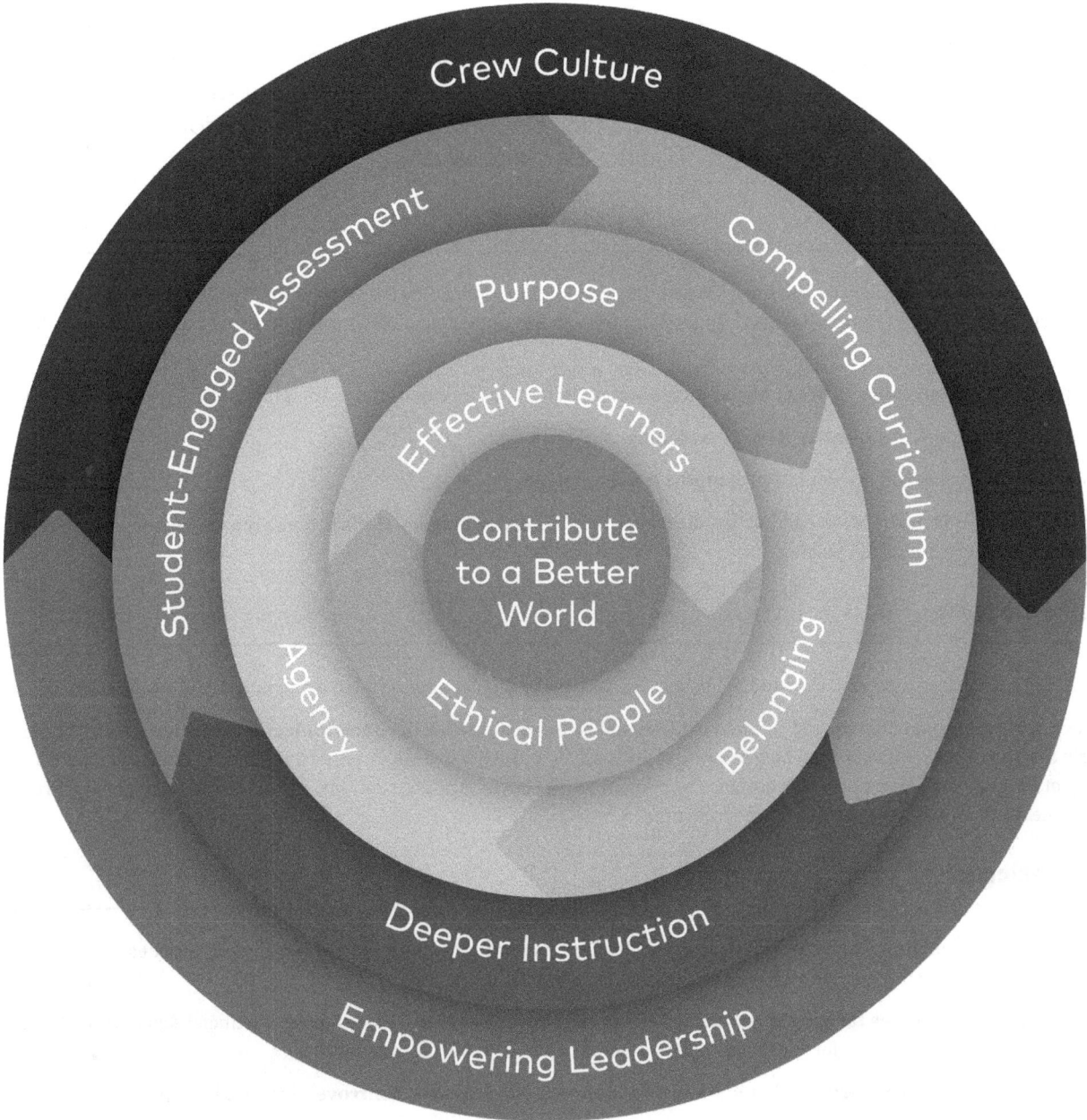

Concentric circle diagram. From outermost to innermost: Crew Culture; Compelling Curriculum; Deeper Instruction; Empowering Leadership; Student-Engaged Assessment; Purpose; Belonging; Agency; Effective Learners; Ethical People; center: Contribute to a Better World

Attributes of High-Quality Student Work

The descriptions below are intended to provide educators with common vision and terminology as they engage in using student work to improve teaching and learning, be it shorter task work or products that are the result of long-term projects. These attributes are not intended to constrain a conversation about quality, and not all descriptors must be present for a piece of work to be high quality. They are intended to provoke deeper conversation and act as a starting point for formulating a shared understanding of quality. These descriptions align with EL Core Practices 5 (Designing Projects and Products) and 7 (Producing High-Quality Student Work).

Complexity

- Complex work is rigorous: it aligns with or exceeds the expectations defined by grade-level standards and includes **higher-order thinking** by challenging students to apply, analyze, evaluate, and create during daily instruction and throughout longer projects.

- Complex work often **connects to the big concepts** that undergird disciplines or unite disciplines.

- Complex work prioritizes **transfer of understanding** to new contexts.

- Complex work prioritizes consideration of **multiple perspective**s.

- Complex work may incorporate students' **application of higher order literacy skills** through the use of complex text and evidence-based writing and speaking.

Craftsmanship

- Well-crafted work is done with care and precision. Craftsmanship requires attention to **accuracy, detail, and beauty**.

- In every discipline and domain, well-crafted work should be **beautiful work in conception and execution**. In short tasks or early drafts of work, craftsmanship may be present primarily in thoughtful ideas, but not in polished presentation; for long-term projects, craftsmanship requires perseverance to refine work in conception, conventions, and presentation, typically through multiple drafts or rehearsals with critique from others.

Authenticity

- Authentic work demonstrates the **original, creative thinking of students**—authentic personal voice and ideas—rather than simply showing that students can follow directions or fill in the blanks.

- Authentic work often **uses formats and standards from the professional world**, rather than artificial school formats (e.g., students create a book review for a local newspaper instead of a book report for the teacher).

- Authentic work **often connects academic standards with real-world issues, controversies, and local people and places**.

- Authenticity gives purpose to work; the **work matters to students and ideally contributes to a larger community** as well. When possible, it is created for and shared with an audience beyond the classroom.

EL Education Core Practices

Our Core Practices address five key domains of life in school.

Curriculum	EL Education's approach to curriculum promotes both challenge and joy in learning. We encourage educators to use, adapt, or design curricula that allow all students to grapple with demanding, standards-based content and meaningful tasks and produce high-quality work. We believe curricula should elevate student collaboration, voice, thinking, and reflection; should reflect a commitment to developing character; and should empower students to contribute to a more just and equitable world.
Instruction	EL Education promotes instruction that is alive with discovery, inquiry, critical thinking, problem solving, and collaboration. Teachers talk less. Students talk and think more. Lessons challenge, engage, and empower students with complex issues, text, and problems. They lift up big disciplinary ideas and give students practice with the tools and skills professionals use in the real world as they create high-quality work. Teachers differentiate instruction and empower all students to be self-directed, independent learners.
Culture and Character	The EL Education model fosters and celebrates students' character development by building a culture in which students and staff work together to become effective learners and ethical people who contribute to a better world. Schools establish Habits of Character—qualities like respect, responsibility, courage, and kindness—and model and discuss them every day. The school is suffused by a spirit of crew: students and staff work together as a team to sustain a learning community where everyone belongs and can succeed.
Student-Engaged Assessment	EL Education believes that assessment practices should motivate students to become leaders of their own learning. Students track their progress toward standards-based learning targets, set goals, and reflect on growth and challenges. Students and teachers regularly analyze quantitative and qualitative data that include assessments, reflections, and student work and use those data to inform goals and instruction. Students regularly present evidence of their achievement and growth through student-led family conferences, passage presentations, and celebrations of learning.
Leadership	EL Education supports school leaders to build a cohesive school vision focused on EL Education's Dimensions of Student Achievement, continuous improvement, and shared leadership. Leaders align resources and activities to the school's vision and lead a professional culture with a growth mindset. Leaders shape school structures to provide equitable education to all students, celebrate joy in learning, and build a schoolwide learning community of trust and collaboration. Leaders work collaboratively with families, staff, and students to make evidence-based decisions that enable all students to achieve.

Curriculum

EL Education's approach to curriculum promotes both challenge and joy in learning. We encourage educators to use, adapt, or design curricula that allow all students to grapple with demanding, standards-based content and meaningful tasks and produce high-quality work. We believe curricula should elevate student collaboration, voice, thinking, and reflection; should reflect a commitment to developing character; and should empower students to contribute to a more just and equitable world.

In the Curriculum domain, we provide guidance for schools and teachers who are choosing, adapting, or enhancing a published curriculum and for those who are designing their own.

Core Practices in This Domain

• Choosing, Adapting, and Enhancing Curricula

• Mapping Knowledge, Skills, and Habits of Character

• Supporting College and Career Readiness

• Supporting Global Citizenship

• Supporting Social, Emotional, and Physical Wellness

• Designing Case Studies

• Incorporating Fieldwork, Experts, and Service Learning

• Designing Projects and Products

• Designing Learning Expeditions

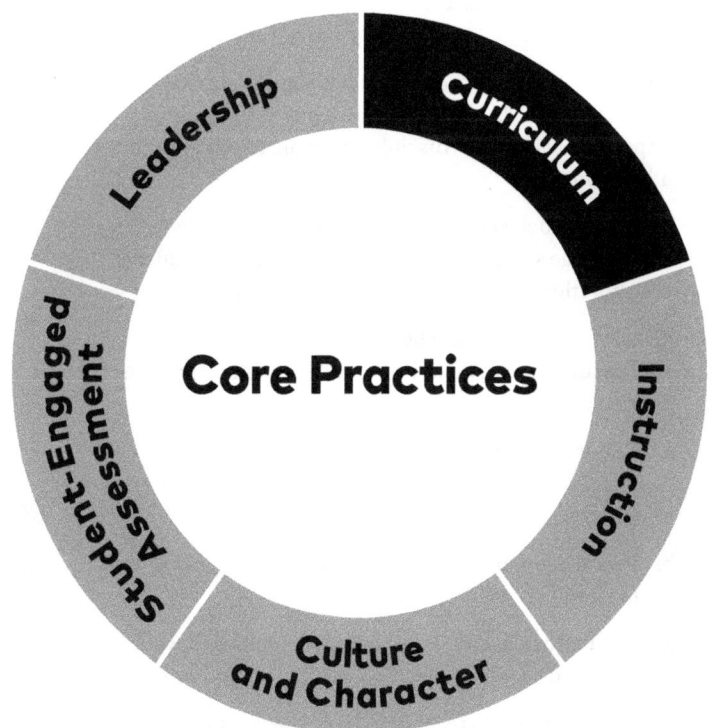

Core Practice 1

Choosing, Adapting, and Enhancing Curricula

EL Education supports districts and schools that choose, adapt, or enhance published curricula as well as those that design their own curricula. This Core Practice addresses the use of published curricula.

When districts or schools choose published curricula, they do so in order to give all students access to challenging content and engaging lessons that prepare them for college, careers, and global citizenship. Classrooms are dynamic systems that require responsiveness and flexibility. Therefore, it is sometimes appropriate to adapt or enhance a curriculum while maintaining fidelity to standards and the integrity of the curriculum's aims and methods. Adaptation or enhancement can be a wise choice if it increases students' understanding of content, elevates challenge, addresses needed literacy or numeracy skills, and builds student engagement.

Notes:

1) Teacher-designed curricula and enhancements that engage students through case studies; projects and products; fieldwork, experts, and service learning; and learning expeditions will be addressed in Core Practices 6–10.

2) There are many other considerations for choosing curricula, such as cost, technical support, or format, that we do not address in these Core Practices.

A. Choosing Published Curricula

1. District, school, and teacher leaders choose (adopt) curricula that are research-based and supported by credible data that demonstrate student achievement. EL Education defines student achievement as mastery of knowledge and skills, character, and high-quality student work.

2. District, school, and teacher leaders choose curricula that are standards-aligned and sequenced to maximize opportunities for interdisciplinary connections and vertical alignment.

3. District, school, and teacher leaders choose curricula that provide structures and protocols to elevate student collaboration, voice, thinking, and reflection.

4. District, school, and teacher leaders choose curricula that ensure equity and access for all students. Equitable curricula:

   a. Feature texts, problems, or activities that promote multiple perspectives and understanding of multiple cultures

   b. Describe opportunities for differentiating lessons to meet the needs of all students

   c. Ensure that all students have opportunities to work with rigorous grade-level content, texts, and problems

5. District, school, and teacher leaders choose curricula that invite students to explore global studies, environmental stewardship, and topics that address equity and social justice. Such topics can engage students in compelling discussions of right and wrong.

6. District, school, and teacher leaders choose curricula that promote strong Habits of Character and create opportunities for students to practice academic courage, perseverance, collaboration, responsibility for learning, and service to their communities.

7. District, school, and teacher leaders ensure that the integration of technology as a learning tool is built into the curricula to equip all students with professional competencies such as media literacy and technology-assisted research.

8. District, school, and teacher leaders periodically review measures of student achievement to determine how well the curriculum is addressing standards. They make adjustments to curriculum maps to ensure that students are challenged and engaged and that repetition is minimized.

B. Adapting Published Curricula

1. When school and teacher leaders strategically select and adapt parts of a published curriculum, they do so to increase the challenge or engagement for students. The goal of adaptation is to maintain the integrity of the curriculum within the unique context of a particular class or school. It should be undertaken with deep intention and

a careful, deliberate process for review and adjustment of materials and lessons.

2. School and teacher leaders analyze a published curriculum for the logic of its design and flow. They ask:

   a. How does this curriculum scaffold students' knowledge and skills through the year to prepare them for the next grade?

   b. What skills and knowledge do students learn in the first parts of the curriculum that are essential for tackling the rest of the curriculum?

   c. How does the complexity of the texts, problems, and tasks included in the curriculum match the grade level being taught and the standards students are expected to meet?

   d. What is the arc of the units and lessons in the curriculum? What lessons and assessments need to occur as written to achieve the goals of the curriculum?

   e. What guidance does the curriculum offer for differentiation? What additional scaffolds could be prepared to adjust the curriculum for students with learning disabilities or those who need more challenge?

   f. What key structures (e.g., instructional routines, discussions, use of note-catchers, anchor charts) are critical to scaffold student success?

3. School and teacher leaders, based on their review, identify the specific aspects of the published curricula they will use or adapt. For example, if the curriculum is designed to address content standards not aligned to the school's own state standards, school and teacher leaders may choose to use only the parts that align with required standards.

4. When adapting parts but not all of a curriculum, leaders and teachers communicate and collaborate across grade levels and subject areas to avoid redundancy and build cohesion that ensures all students master required knowledge and skills.

5. Teachers and specialists articulate and enhance the scaffolding or extensions for students who require more challenge, English language learners, or students with disabilities.

6. Teachers augment a task in an existing curriculum only if the revised task achieves the same learning targets and enhances student engagement or authenticity (e.g., transforming a textbook task with generic information into a real-world task with specific, local information to make it more authentic for students).

C. Enhancing Curricula with Supplementary Materials and Opportunities

1. Teachers add texts to those associated with a curriculum for purposes that include:

   a) Increasing the complexity or challenge of the text

   b) Connecting to a current event or local topic of interest to students

   c) Creating more accessible reading related to the topic of study for particular students (e.g., easier reading as a supplement, not substitute, for complex text)

2. Teachers may choose to enhance curricula with media that provide a local, current, or alternative perspective; create opportunities for students to gather information digitally; or illustrate particular concepts relevant to the curricula.

3. Teachers may choose to supplement curricula with games or manipulatives that create opportunities for students to engage, explore, and apply concepts kinesthetically.

Core Practice 2

Mapping Knowledge, Skills, and Habits of Character

In the EL Education model, teachers and school leaders collaborate to ensure that schoolwide, standards-aligned curriculum maps act as the foundation for all planning, instruction, and assessment. Curriculum maps describe a vertical sequence of academic and character targets that are to be addressed at each grade level and within each discipline. These targets become increasingly more sophisticated and rigorous as students progress through the grades. Curriculum maps also provide a year-at-a-glance view of what's being taught and assessed across disciplines. They guard against unnecessary repetition of content across grades and ensure appropriate repetition of knowledge, skills, and Habits of Character as students move up through the grades.

Leaders and teachers map required standards and college readiness skills to document instruction that has already happened and revise annually to plan instruction for the upcoming year. They include learning targets, texts, topics, and tasks in their maps. They articulate the progression of interdisciplinary learning expeditions, case studies, and projects through the school year in a particular grade and spiraling up through the grade levels, as well as the disciplinary content that is taught outside of learning expeditions.

A. Standards Alignment

1. Teachers and leaders prioritize standards that will receive particular emphasis, creating opportunities for depth and repeated practice of key skills and concepts.

2. For curricula designed by the school, teachers and leaders bundle key standards into complementary interdisciplinary sets that serve as a spine for projects, case studies, and learning expeditions.

3. Teachers and leaders chunk curriculum maps by marking period so that teachers are able to reach a certain level of closure on specific standards within a term. This supports alignment between curriculum pacing and standards-based grading.

B. Mapping Learning Targets

1. For learning expeditions, teachers and leaders create one cohesive map that aligns standards-based academic and character learning targets across all involved disciplines. In schools where all or most standards are being taught through learning expeditions, these will be the primary curriculum maps.

2. Teachers and leaders map standards covered outside of learning expeditions (e.g., during daily mathematics class or content-specific courses in secondary schools or when students are not "on expedition") to show when knowledge, skills, and Habits of Character are taught and how they are assessed.

3. Teachers and leaders sequence learning targets to maximize interdisciplinary connections whenever possible. For example, in language arts, students may have the target, "I can make inferences about character motivations in *The Grapes of Wrath*." In social studies, the same students may have the target, "I can explain how weather and agricultural practices contributed to the Dust Bowl."

4. Teachers and leaders sequence learning targets to support and scaffold tasks and products. For example, students working on a research paper may begin with skill targets focused on identifying accurate and reliable sources, then address note-taking targets, then writing targets, and finally revision targets.

5. Teachers and leaders map character learning targets to reflect the school's Habits of Character. They create opportunities for students to focus on and demonstrate progress toward behaviors that enable them to be effective learners and ethical people.

C. Mapping Texts, Tasks, and Assessments

1. Teachers and leaders identify anchor texts and other complex texts (both primary and secondary sources) for content topics that leverage literacy standards across the curriculum.

2. Teachers and leaders articulate the major tasks that students will do to make progress toward long-term learning targets, including priority writing standards for each marking period. This helps teachers and leaders monitor the variety and complexity in product format over time. (Performance tasks, such as student writing or other products, that are highly scaffolded and revised multiple times are not sufficient assessments of knowledge or skills but can be strong measures of students' quality of work and Habits of Character).

3. Teachers and leaders identify formative assessments (e.g., lab notebooks, reading journals), summative assessments (e.g., mathematics unit tests), and on-demand assessments (e.g., on-demand writing) of discrete long-term targets.

Core Practice 3

Supporting College and Career Readiness

The EL Education model prepares all students for college and career success by providing a college-bound curriculum with high expectations for all students, fostering a schoolwide college- and career-bound culture, and setting up structures that allow time for the post-graduation search and application process.

A college-bound curriculum includes content area knowledge and skills, such as literature and calculus, academic research and writing skills, and technology literacy. Creating high-quality work, including finished, professional-looking products, is an essential part of core and enrichment courses that prepare all students for college and careers. Habits of Scholarship, such as time management, persistence toward excellence, and "college knowledge" about such things as college admissions, financial aid requirements, and the norms and expectations of diverse college environments are also part of a college-bound curriculum. Paving the way for college and careers begins in the primary years and culminates with intensive focus in the high school years.

EL Education recognizes that there may be particular students for whom entering college may not be the optimal path. School leaders and teachers support all students to explore postsecondary options that best fit their interests and needs. They prepare all students to get accepted to college so that they have a choice now and the confidence to reapply in the future if college is the right option.

A. Promoting College-Bound Curricula

1. Teachers and leaders provide students of all ages with opportunities to develop the Habits of Character (e.g., self-management, collaboration, perseverance) that they will need to navigate the academic and social demands of college. They explicitly and continuously focus on Habits of Character in Crew.

2. Teachers in every subject area and at all grade levels teach the research skills and analytic thinking that will prepare students for the evidence-based approach of college courses.

3. Teachers in every subject area and at all grade levels teach literacy to prepare students for the complexity of texts and volume of reading and writing in college.

4. Teachers and leaders create a course schedule that gives K–8 students access to the courses and opportunities that prepare them for a college-bound high school curriculum (e.g., eighth-grade algebra, world language).

5. Teachers provide students with identified disabilities appropriate differentiated instruction, accommodations, and support to help them succeed in college preparatory courses, or differentiated guidance to help them explore appropriate work and self-supporting options after high school.

6. Leaders create a course schedule that ensures all high school students take a demanding college preparatory curriculum that is aligned to college admission requirements.

B. Building College- and Career-Ready Skills

1. School leaders, classroom and Crew teachers, and school counselors offer opportunities for students to learn about a variety of careers and the skills and habits individuals need to thrive in the workplace. For example, they hold career fairs, invite experts to share their work experiences, and encourage students to interview workers in fields of interest to them.

2. School leaders, classroom and Crew teachers, and school counselors help students explore and acquire internships that allow students to acquire work experience and learn about career opportunities and the education required to be successful in 21st-century fields.

3. Teachers ensure that technology literacy is woven throughout all subject areas and grade levels whenever resources allow. Enhancing technology literacy includes:

   a. Providing students with new technologies (e.g., design and presentation software, social networking) to access and manage information and prepare for success in a knowledge economy

   b. Teaching students the ethical and legal issues surrounding access to and use of technology

   c. Providing technology as a tool for original research that enables students to produce high-quality products, performances, and presentations

   d. Maintaining high standards for the quality of work produced using technology.

e. Establishing learning targets for the technology skills (e.g., effective use of spreadsheet or presentation software) that are distinct from learning targets for the quality of thinking and content presented in the project

4. Teachers capitalize on the ubiquitous availability of information sources to support high-quality student work. They ensure that internet technologies are used with scholarly integrity and insight (e.g., that web content sources are analyzed for validity, used wisely, and properly cited).

5. Teachers take advantage of technological innovations to support students in making things with their own hands (e.g., a robotics project that introduces physics concepts) and sometimes to extend student project work beyond the school day and the school building (e.g., making a film in a studio, using a scientific instrument in a professional lab).

6. As resources allow, teachers and leaders provide students with opportunities to learn creative and technical skills such as carpentry, music production, or engineering. (Technical skills may take the form of coursework or apprenticeships that enable a student to learn a craft or discipline).

C. Structures to Support College and Career Readiness

1. School leaders, classroom and Crew teachers, and school counselors create a college-bound culture in which all students are on a path to college and meaningful careers by:

    a. Displaying college symbols and messages in hallways, classrooms, and offices

    b. Providing opportunities to visit college campuses—starting in sixth grade if possible

    c. Teaching high school students the facts about applying for admission and financial aid and about the norms and culture of college life

    d. Inviting alumni to the school to serve as mentors and resources

    e. Discussing college at schoolwide events

    f. Promoting college resources on the school's website and other publications

    g. Celebrating college acceptances in classrooms, in Crews, and at schoolwide events

    h. Identifying and publicizing college-bound opportunities for specific populations of students (e.g., first-generation students, students of color)

2. School counselors and high school Crew teachers help students make strong course selections that are connected to college and career aspirations, monitor progress toward academic and character learning targets, and work to explore college options and navigate applications for admission, financial aid, and scholarships.

3. School counselors and/or Crew teachers invite guest speakers (e.g., recent alumni who are attending college, young working professionals, college admissions officers) to build student understanding of post-graduation life and the academic and character expectations of diverse college environments.

4. High school leaders schedule intensive classes that provide remediation for those students who need it or content-rich extracurricular opportunities for those meeting learning targets in their regular course work.

5. When appropriate for individual students, school counselors and teachers explore the value of gap-year and other post-graduation work/learning experiences that enable students to mature and build the self-directed skills that provide a doorway into college and career success.

6. School counselors and teachers educate students and families about how to maximize students' chances of college admission by maintaining a strong high school transcript, engaging in extracurricular leadership, taking required college admissions tests, etc.

7. School counselors and teachers offer evening sessions on such topics as choosing the right college and filling in financial aid applications, particularly to support parents with first-generation college applicants.

8. Leaders and teachers design graduation traditions that showcase students' accomplishment in EL Education's Dimensions of Student Achievement and provide both motivation and affirmation at the end of students' K–12 academic career.

Core Practice 4
Supporting Global Citizenship

In the EL Education model, leaders and teachers recognize that they must prepare students for global citizenship in an increasingly complicated and interconnected world and that multilingualism is a key tool and a vital global skill that deepens understanding of other countries and cultures. Curricula that prepare students for global citizenship are cross-disciplinary and include developing knowledge of diverse cultures, languages, and political systems, as well as knowledge of the physical terrains, ecosystems, and natural forces of the planet. Fully integrating global skills and knowledge into the curriculum is tied closely to environmental stewardship and social justice as students are challenged to grapple with the most complex problems facing the world (such as climate change, structures of economic inequities, and international terrorism and conflict). Teachers also ask students to discover and attend to how others see themselves, their histories, and the world's problems that is, to hear and analyze multiple perspectives along the way to determining what young people can do to make a difference.

A. Choosing or Creating Curricula That Support Global Skills and Knowledge

1. Teachers and leaders review curriculum maps to ensure that global knowledge and skills (e.g., knowledge of diverse cultures, world geography, speaking a second language) are reflected in curriculum maps.

2. Teachers and leaders choose or design curricula that enable students to thoughtfully explore multiple perspectives and cultures, as well as issues of equity and diversity.

3. Teachers and leaders create interdisciplinary curricula that provide multiple opportunities for students to build global skills and knowledge (e.g., a case study on Cesar Chavez co-taught in Spanish and language arts class, with some lessons conducted in Spanish, or a learning expedition that analyzes the consequences of climate change from different international perspectives).

B. Building Character through Global Citizenship

1. Teachers and leaders teach Habits of Character that guide students in becoming global citizens and enable them to value different perspectives and opportunities to learn from and contribute to diverse cultures (e.g., service, empathy).

2. Teachers and Crew leaders design lessons that enable students to value and strive for diversity, inclusion, and equity.

3. Teachers, leaders, and Crew leaders design learning experiences that enable students to make concrete contributions to the world around them.

C. Supporting Multilingualism

1. Teachers support all students in acquiring English language. They simultaneously incorporate and build classroom and schoolwide traditions on the perspectives, experiences, and insights of students from different countries and cultures. (They value the resource of knowledge and skills that students who speak languages other than English bring to classrooms and the school.)

2. School leaders create a schedule that enables all students to study at least one language other than English by the time they graduate from high school. They make world language learning a central part of the curriculum at all levels of instruction and begin world language instruction as early as possible with young learners.

3. Leaders create a schedule that offers world languages in extended, well-articulated sequences that develop increasing levels of proficiency at each level of instruction by teachers who are well qualified in language proficiency, cultural knowledge, and teaching skills.

4. As much as possible, teachers enhance world language learning by connecting students with cultural and artistic opportunities and empowering them to contribute to the community and the school.

Core Practice 5

Promoting Social, Emotional, and Physical Wellness

The EL Education model promotes social, emotional, mental, and physical health and wellness throughout the curriculum and schoolwide culture. Schools choose curricula that promote character development through social and emotional learning, a healthy relationship with the outdoors, and physical challenge. Healthy relationships, growth mindset, intellectual courage, exercise, stress reduction, sleep, spending time outdoors—the key elements of physical and mental health—are all included in a school's wellness approach.

Experiences in the outdoors—playing in, learning from, and appreciating nature, including on school or city playgrounds and during fieldwork in city neighborhoods—are a priority for EL Education. Whenever possible and appropriate, students are encouraged to be active and outdoors during the school day.

Crews emphasize the importance of wellness and teach explicit lessons to support wellness. The physical education program emphasizes personal fitness, self-care, inclusion of diverse abilities, and challenge by choice as well as competitive sports. Good sportsmanship, collaboration, health, and growth in fitness are emphasized over a win-at-all-costs mentality.

A. Incorporating Wellness into Curricula

1. School leaders and teachers align disciplinary standards and learning expedition topics with wellness goals. They use physical education classes, Crew, learning expeditions, case studies, and projects to teach and model wellness.

2. When adapting or enhancing curricula, selecting case studies, or designing projects or learning expeditions, teachers may include wellness as a focus of study or a product of the learning (e.g., a project researching nutrition costs and benefits in the school cafeteria as part of a broader study of health and the food economy; a proposal for bike lanes on neighborhood streets written by students).

3. Leaders, school counselors, and teachers create Crew lessons that promote social and emotional safety and health. Wellness is an explicit focus of Crew curriculum and instruction.

    a. Crew leaders create a climate of social and emotional safety for students.

    b. Crew leaders explicitly support students to understand and monitor dangers to wellness posed by alcohol, drugs, and tobacco, as well as overuse of technological devices.

4. Leaders ensure that outdoor education programs as well as individual and team sports promote health, wellness, and character development through adventure and good sportsmanship. They celebrate collaboration with teammates and personal bests, as well as competing fairly against opponents.

B. Creating a Culture of Wellness

1. Leaders establish policies and protocols to ensure that physical education classes, adventure programming, and fieldwork are physically and emotionally safe.

2. Leaders and teachers develop extracurricular options (clubs, support groups) that focus on wellness. They establish traditions and events (fund-raisers, community circles, schoolwide challenges) to promote and celebrate students' social and emotional health.

3. Leaders establish practices that limit the availability of unhealthy foods (e.g., soda, candy) and provide healthy and attractive alternatives.

4. Leaders and teachers promote wellness through modeling and instruction in many aspects of physical and mental health, including food, exercise, sleep, spending time in nature, and mindfulness. Teachers and Crew leaders engage students in understanding and addressing health risks.

5. All teachers promote wellness through active breaks, multisensory instruction, and classroom management that demonstrates awareness of students' mental health.

6. All teachers include active and reflective outdoor time for students whenever possible and appropriate. This energizes students' minds and bodies and encourages enjoyment of the outdoors.

7. Classroom, Crew, and physical education teachers encourage students to take on physical challenges, stretching beyond their comfort zones when it comes to

Promoting Social, Emotional, and Physical Wellness (continued)

fitness and adventure. Challenge by choice, with support from a nonjudgmental Crew, is the norm in classrooms and the school. This does not mean that students can choose not to participate. It means that they are encouraged to articulate and choose the kind of participation that is challenging for them (walking around the track instead of running).

8. Teachers craft wellness learning targets and assessments that create opportunities for students to track their progress toward increased teamwork, self-management, and perseverance. They provide kind, specific, and helpful feedback and celebrate students' improvements individually and collectively.

9. Physical education teachers focus on students' strengths and differentiate for their individual needs so that all students can experience success in improving fitness and wellness.

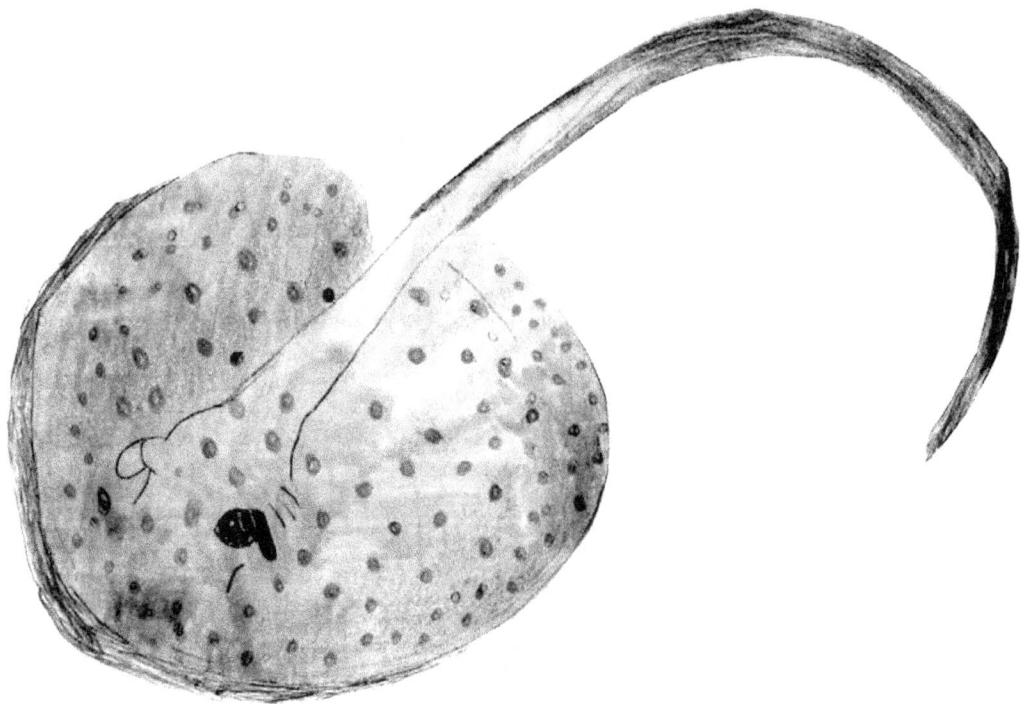

Core Practice 6
Designing Case Studies

In the EL Education model, the term "case study" means two things. First, it is *an approach* to research: using a narrowed topic as a window into big ideas and concepts. This kind of case study is usually incorporated into projects and learning expeditions. Second, a case study can be *a structure* itself, outside of a project or learning expedition—a focused investigation that does not require (as a project does) a culminating product.

Sometimes, EL Education uses the term "case study" exactly as it is applied in the fields of law, business, or medicine, to refer to an investigation of a unique person, place, institution, or event (e.g., a study of inventors, including a case study of Thomas Edison; a study of race in America, including a case study of race in 1960s Milwaukee). Other times, EL uses the term more loosely, to refer to a narrowed subtopic that allows students to focus their research on a particular category (e.g., the topic of birds narrowed to a case study of owls; a study of the Civil War, narrowed to a case study of children in the war) or to compare different perspectives (e.g., historical and current, local and international, scientific and historical, literary and real-life). In both uses, a case study helps students focus their research and become experts on a specific topic before they generalize their learning to broader concepts and content.

Case studies are typically, but not always, 2 to 6 weeks in duration

A. Selecting Case Studies

1. Teachers choose case study topics based on priority standards for which there are ample resources that will allow students to deeply explore a narrow topic and become experts.

2. Teachers choose case study topics that enliven content and concepts through a lens that is engaging to students (e.g., a scientific study of the water cycle brought to life by a case study of the city's water supply).

3. Teachers choose case studies that allow students to engage in original research with primary source materials just as professional historians, mathematicians, scientists, and writers would.

4. Whenever possible, teachers choose case studies that focus on local issues and use local resources to help students make connections between their academic learning and the real world and build bridges between the school and local community.

B. Designing Case Studies

1. Teachers infuse case studies with literacy—reading, writing, speaking, listening, research, and vocabulary development. They infuse mathematics when there is a genuine and strategic fit.

2. Teachers prioritize the use of primary source text and data to ground research in the real world, promote discovery, and challenge students as readers and mathematicians (e.g., reading an actual police report during a case study of

an incident). These texts and data, often from local sources or experts, are used for explicit instruction in literacy and mathematical skills.

3. Teachers guide students to generalize from case studies, applying their understanding to the broader knowledge and skills required by standards.

4. Teachers often begin designing learning expeditions by using a single case study and later build on two or three case studies to provide multiple perspectives. Projects sometimes align with a single case study and other times cut across multiple case studies.

5. Case studies may be part of a project that results in a product but may also stand alone without a culminating product.

Core Practice 7

Incorporating Fieldwork, Experts, and Service Learning

The EL Education model connects students to the world beyond school through meaningful fieldwork, collaboration with experts, and service learning. In addition to learning from text and classroom-based experiences, students use the natural and social environments of their communities as sites for purposeful fieldwork and service connected to academic work. They collaborate with professional experts and community members with firsthand knowledge of events and issues to ensure accuracy, integrity, and quality in their work.

EL Education differentiates between traditional field trips, in which students are often spectators, and fieldwork, in which students are active investigators, applying the research tools, techniques of inquiry, and standards of presentation used by professionals in the field.

Service learning goes beyond charitable acts, such as cleaning up a city park, and extends also to rigorous academic products that provide a service for the community, such as energy audits of city buildings that help a city save money and reduce its carbon footprint.

Fieldwork, collaboration with experts, and service learning are integral parts of learning expeditions, but they can also be used to enhance published curriculum or as stand-alone structures outside of full learning expeditions.

A. Planning and Designing Fieldwork

1. Teachers identify and plan for rich fieldwork experiences that have a clear purpose connected to the curriculum. They prepare note-catchers, procedures, or activities that allow students to be researchers, not spectators.

2. When time and resources allow, teachers schedule fieldwork over an extended period of time with several visits to the same site.

3. Teachers instruct students in procedures and skills for fieldwork before setting out or during the first visit. They create a foundation for all students to be engaged and purposeful.

4. As much as possible, teachers design fieldwork experiences based on the authentic research of professionals in the field (e.g., zoologists, historians, anthropologists).

5. Teachers select data collection tools to suit the purpose of the fieldwork. When data are collected, they are analyzed and used back in the classroom to create a product.

6. Teachers structure fieldwork so that it is safe and productive. Teachers preview sites to shape the field experience effectively and ensure accessibility for all students.

7. Leaders and teachers establish written policies and well-documented safety procedures for conducting fieldwork. These include planning for the logistics of transportation, grouping students, and adult supervision.

8. Teachers prepare students to be ambassadors for their school. Students are courteous, knowledgeable, organized, and helpful during fieldwork experiences.

9. In schools where there are barriers to transporting students off campus, teachers and leaders seek creative options for fieldwork, such as selecting case studies that can be authentically explored through on-campus fieldwork (e.g., bacteria growth in public spaces, invasive species on campus, conducting a schoolwide survey).

10. Whenever possible, teachers look for opportunities to enhance published curricula with fieldwork experiences that deepen learning for students.

B. Selecting and Engaging with Experts

1. Teachers bring experts from the community into the classroom to collaborate with students on projects, teach them skills from their field, and critique their work using professional standards.

2. Teachers reach out to experts who represent multiple perspectives and backgrounds and can expand students' understanding of the knowledge and skills they are seeking to acquire. Experts may be professionals from a particular discipline or community members with firsthand knowledge of the topic being studied.

3. Teachers prepare experts to work collaboratively with students on projects and/or products. For example, experts may help students critique their work against professional standards.

4. Teachers prepare students to greet experts with courtesy, respect, and background knowledge, with the desire that experts are surprised and delighted by the students' depth of knowledge and preparation.

5. Teachers and students orient experts to the needs of the project and the protocols for class critique.

6. Teachers support students to maintain ongoing relationships with experts. For example, teachers help students take a lead role in communication with experts before (to ensure alignment and focus), during (to keep the collaboration on track), and after (showing appreciation or sharing their work) a visit.

C. Designing and Planning Service Learning

1. Teachers incorporate service learning into projects and lessons not as an afterthought or add-on, but as an integral part of learning.

   a. Teachers connect service learning to the ethic of kindness and service that is part of school culture.

   b. Teachers use service as a prime vehicle to teach and take action centered on social justice and to address the challenges and celebrate the assets of living in community.

   c. Teachers and students research service opportunities to ensure that service learning projects provide a real benefit to the community.

2. Teachers design and plan service learning experiences that go beyond charitable volunteer work to include projects that build important *academic* skills. These experiences help students to see that academic work can be in the service of good for others (e.g., building literacy skills by collaborating with homeless shelter residents to create a guide to free city services).

Core Practice 8
Designing Projects and Products

In the EL Education model, teachers engage students in skills- and knowledge-rich learning experiences (projects) that result in high-quality products or performances for audiences beyond the classroom. EL Education defines a project as not just the tangible product resulting from learning, but as the series of classroom lessons, discussions, labs, work sessions, student research, and fieldwork that provide an in-school structure for teaching core skills and content. Projects are used to teach literacy, mathematics, and other disciplinary content and skills, as well as collaboration and problem solving.

The products of student projects are typically modeled after professional work. Whenever possible, products are critiqued by professionals and contribute to an audience beyond the classroom community. Projects can also culminate in a performance, event, or presentation (e.g., a symposium on a local health issue; an original historical play).

Teachers check for mastery of knowledge and skills throughout the project, and students track their progress toward learning targets. Students' knowledge and skills are assessed through ongoing measures (e.g., daily work, tests, journals, observations, on-demand tasks, and writing assessments). Final products and performances, which are highly scaffolded, are assessed for craftsmanship and Habits of Character such as perseverance and collaboration.

Projects are part of learning expeditions and can also be stand-alone structures outside of full learning expeditions. They may be aligned with a single case study or cut across multiple case studies.

Projects are typically, but not always, 2 to 6 weeks in duration.

A. Designing Projects

1. Teachers design projects as a central structure for learning standards-aligned knowledge and skills during the school day (not as an enrichment when core learning is done). Projects culminate in something of value shared with an audience beyond the classroom: a product (e.g., scientific report, book, museum exhibit, machine) or a performance.

2. Teachers plan backward from the final student product or performance. Lessons, labs, research, fieldwork, experts, and product creation, as well as regular assessments, are scheduled to lead up to the completion of a high-quality culminating piece, planned with the audience in mind.

3. Teachers craft learning targets for the project that include standards-aligned academic and character targets.

4. Teachers weave literacy into every stage of the project (e.g., reading and research to build understanding; speaking and listening to analyze perspectives and formulate ideas; writing for a particular purpose and audience). Literacy includes close reading of complex text and independent reading or research.

5. Teachers evaluate and choose project-related texts that will allow students to build knowledge from rich informational and/or literary texts.

a. Teachers select anchor texts that offer multiple perspectives on the topic and opportunities to learn domain-specific and academic vocabulary, as well as disciplinary conventions.

b. Teachers select mentor texts that model the craft, genre, or format students will be using in their own products.

6. Teachers weave mathematics into projects when it is a genuine and strategic fit. Teachers seek out primary source data and/or build data sets with students and teach specific mathematical skills and concepts through those data as part of the project.

7. Teachers involve students as much as possible in directing aspects of the project, with clear, posted, student-monitored organizational structures (e.g., learning targets, calendars, checklists, rubrics) that help students hold themselves and others accountable for their individual and group progress.

8. Teachers assess progress toward learning targets during all aspects of the project, not just at the completion of the final product. The project includes formative and summative assessments such as conferences, quizzes, tests, short written responses, and essays to give students many opportunities to practice and gain confidence in both knowledge and skills before creating a final product.

9. Teachers debrief lessons to guide students to generalize from and synthesize concepts they've learned in projects so that the learning can be transferred to other settings.

B. Planning Products and Performances

1. Teachers plan products and performances for an audience beyond the classroom, giving students an authentic reason to care about quality.

2. Teachers craft product descriptors and assignments that clearly articulate expectations, including learning targets, criteria, and rubrics that define a successful product and the steps (including deadlines) for planning, revising, and polishing the product over time.

   a. Products and performances are modeled on professional-world formats rather than artificial scholastic formats (e.g., students create a scientific exhibit for a local museum rather than a science poster for the classroom).

   b. Typically, all students work toward the same product format (e.g., scientific report, architectural blueprint, historical play) to engage the power of the classroom community to focus together on the same key skills and format and to support quality through common models of excellence and critique.

   c. Within the common product format, there is room for students to make creative choices (e.g., all students may create architectural blueprints, but students choose the design of their own building).

   d. For group projects, the product is designed so that the work of each student can be evaluated individually, ensuring accountability for all students.

3. Teachers plan lessons and experiences that enable all students to produce high-quality work. Planning for high-quality work includes the following steps:

   a. Identifying professional or student-work models that will help students see what's expected of them

   b. Planning explicit skill lessons that will prepare students to execute the product successfully

   c. Scheduling time that will allow students to complete multiple drafts or rehearsals

   d. Planning critique lessons and feedback protocols

   e. Setting benchmarks for completion of each component or phase in a product to keep students on track

   f. Making some components mandatory for all students and others optional to differentiate instruction for a range of learners

   g. Planning for any technological skills students may need to acquire to be successful in the project (e.g., recording and analyzing data, graphic design, presentation)

4. Teachers design the summative assessment of the final product to focus not on knowledge and skills—which have been assessed during the course of the project—but on the attributes of high-quality work (craftsmanship, complexity, authenticity) and Habits of Character (e.g., perseverance, responsibility for learning). (See also *Core Practice 12: Planning for and Supporting High-Quality Student Work*.)

Core Practice 9
Designing Learning Expeditions

Learning expeditions are the signature EL Education curricular structure. They make standards come alive for students. These long-term, in-depth studies offer real-world connections that inspire students toward higher levels of academic achievement. Learning expeditions involve students in original research, critical thinking, and problem solving, and they build character along with academic skills. All learning expeditions explicitly focus on building literacy skills, particularly in reading and writing informational text and writing from evidence.

Learning expeditions take multiple, powerful elements of the EL model (see Core Practices 6–8) and join them together. All of these structures can also be used independently, outside of full learning expeditions.

Learning expeditions are typically 6 to 12 weeks in duration, though sometimes longer.

A. Planning for the Scope and Components of Learning Expeditions

1. Teachers plan learning expeditions to include the following components: a kickoff experience, guiding questions, one or more projects or case studies that lead to a product, lessons, fieldwork, experts, a culminating event, and often service learning.

2. Teachers plan learning expeditions so that when students are "on expedition," the expedition topic, lessons, and work provide the through-line of their school day across subject areas and, usually, across periods of the day.

   a. In middle and high school classrooms, students may be "on expedition" for a given term in some courses and learning through more traditional disciplinary structures in others. Learning expeditions may be led by a multidisciplinary team or by a single teacher within a subject area that includes interdisciplinary features (i.e., learning expeditions are interdisciplinary, but not necessarily with an equal balance of disciplines).

   b. Learning expeditions integrate skills of reading, writing, listening, speaking, numeracy, and research, as well as critical thinking, problem solving, and collaboration. Explicit literacy instruction, using relevant and appropriately complex text, takes place in learning expeditions at all grade levels.

B. Planning and Refining Learning Expeditions

1. Individual teachers or teaching teams construct or customize learning expeditions.

   a. Teachers design learning expeditions well in advance and begin with the product or performance in mind.

   b. Teachers calendar the components collaboratively and realistically so that students will have time to complete projects and associated products and performances with quality. Whenever possible, they engage students in scheduling and committing to deadlines.

   c. Teachers anticipate that students will take on increasingly more leadership during a learning expedition and that the scope and final product of the expedition may change or expand accordingly.

2. Leaders and teachers create structures for critiquing, revising, and documenting learning expeditions for quality and longevity.

C. Choosing, Focusing, and Unpacking the Compelling Topic

1. Teachers choose learning expedition topics that engage student curiosity and passion by providing opportunities to connect historic, scientific, and other disciplinary concepts to local contexts and specific case studies that make learning more concrete, relevant, and enduring. A compelling topic has the following characteristics:

   a. It is centered on important content standards identified in curriculum maps.

   b. It addresses literacy standards so that students experience the powerful connection between reading about a topic and writing effectively about a topic.

   c. If the topic asks students to apply problem-solving or data analysis skills, it addresses relevant mathematics standards.

   d. It has rich potential for reading complex texts and primary sources from the discipline of study.

   e. It takes a broad content (e.g., the Revolutionary War, Newtonian physics) and focuses it with at least one narrow case study or project that engages students and clarifies concepts (e.g., the role of a local city in the Revolutionary War, the physics of car accidents).

f. It offers strong possibilities for original research and the creation of high-quality products for an authentic audience.

g. It invites students to conduct fieldwork, investigate community resources and issues, and build on their reading knowledge by collecting data, interviewing citizens and experts, and creating products that meet a real community need.

h. It focuses on issues of cultural diversity, equity, social justice, or environmental stewardship. It allows students, in developmentally appropriate ways, to engage in compelling conversations about their ideas of right and wrong.

i. It provides opportunities for students to analyze multiple perspectives, voice their opinions, construct arguments supported by evidence, and serve their communities.

2. Once teachers have identified a compelling topic, they craft one to three guiding questions that do the following:

a. Frame inquiry into the topic and lead students to enduring understanding of broader issues and fundamental concepts within and across disciplines

b. Provide the "so what" and "who cares" for students. Guiding questions help students make connections among lessons, projects, and case studies and see the big picture of their learning

c. Avoid singular "right" answers (e.g., Who were the founders of our nation?) or presuppose a partisan or political stance (e.g., Why should we save Statesville Creek?)

d. Reveal fundamental debates and concepts of a discipline and the essential questions that scholars such as scientists and historians must grapple with in their work (e.g., Whose story is told when history is written?)

e. Are phrased to be student-friendly, age-appropriate, memorable, and thought-provoking (e.g., What is a healthy life?)

f. Can be referred to strategically throughout the learning expedition as students develop increasingly informed and sophisticated responses to these questions, individually and as a group

3. Teachers use the Four T's (Topic, Task, Targets, and Text) framework to strengthen a cohesive learning expedition plan.

a. They identify a compelling **topic**.

b. They plan challenging, engaging **tasks**, including assessments, that align with the learning targets.

c. They craft learning **targets** for content and skills based on required standards that drive the learning expedition.

d. They choose challenging, engaging **texts** that align with the targets.

4. Teachers document their learning expedition plans and create standards-targets-assessment documents.

D. Planning for the Flow of Learning Expeditions

1. Teachers plan a kickoff or immersion experience for students that ignites curiosity and sparks interest in a topic. The kickoff is designed to:

a. Build background knowledge in the learning expedition content

b. Raise questions rather than answering them

c. End by revealing the guiding questions and an opportunity for students to debrief by forming connections to the questions and brainstorming ways to pursue answers

2. Teachers plan reading, fieldwork, and research experiences that allow students to become experts in the topic. These experiences may include:

a. Building background knowledge through reading primary sources or other texts

b. Interviewing experts who come to the classroom to speak about case study topics

c. Investigating a case study topic through research

d. Conducting laboratory experiments or fieldwork to collect data

3. Teachers plan how students will work on the final product throughout the learning expedition as they acquire and refine their knowledge and skills. This plan includes how and when students will:

a. Take notes and record information needed for the product

b. Make decisions about design and organization of their product

c. Learn skills needed to be successful on the product

d. Draft the product

e. Critique, revise, and polish the final product

4. Teachers plan a culminating event or celebration of learning that features high-quality student work. The plan for presentation includes the following:

a. Logistics that support students to be the main

presenters or docents at the celebration. Students act as teaching experts to explain or perform their work rather than simply displaying it.

b. Time to display student work in a beautiful and professional way that calls attention to craftsmanship and authenticity

c. Drafts of student work and other indicators of the process by which students created their work (e.g., documentation panels that tell the story of the learning and of students' growth and perseverance)

d. Ways for the audience to interact with students by asking questions, providing feedback, or reflecting with students

Instruction

EL Education promotes instruction that is alive with discovery, inquiry, critical thinking, problem solving, and collaboration. Teachers talk less. Students talk and think more. Lessons challenge, engage, and empower students with complex issues, text, and problems. They lift up big disciplinary ideas and give students practice with the tools and skills professionals use in the real world as they create high-quality work. Teachers differentiate instruction and empower all students to be self-directed, independent learners.

Core Practices in This Domain

- Planning Effective Lessons
- Delivering Effective Lessons
- Planning for and Supporting High-Quality Student Work
- Teaching Reading across the Disciplines
- Teaching Writing across the Disciplines
- Teaching Mathematics
- Teaching Science
- Teaching Social Studies
- Teaching in and through the Arts
- Differentiating Instruction
- Teaching English Language Learners

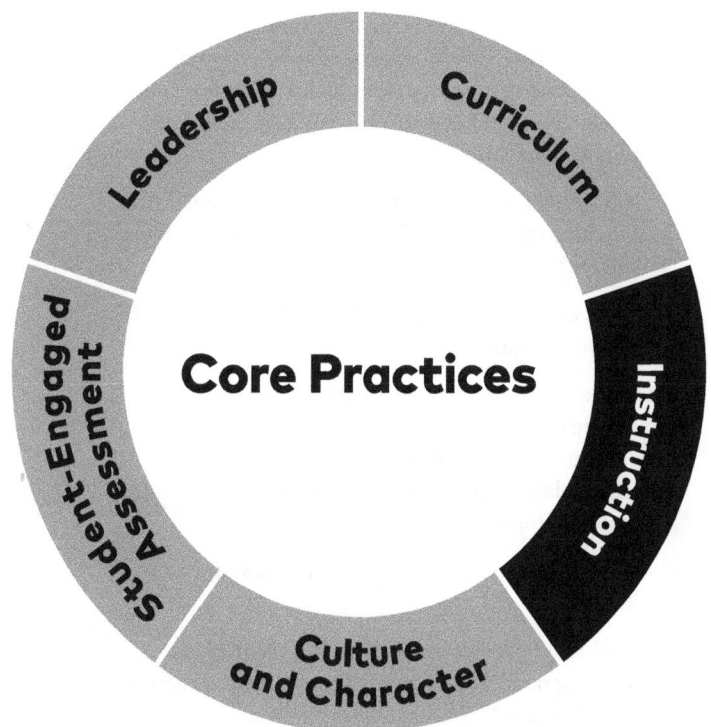

Core Practice 10
Planning Effective Lessons

Lessons are the building blocks of all curricular structures in the EL Education model. Whether planning a single lesson or a series of lessons, teachers attend to how the lessons sit in the larger arc of curriculum. They carefully craft a beginning, middle, and end, regardless of lesson type. By attending to each lesson with care, teachers ensure that all students are challenged, engaged, and empowered and can transfer their understanding to new contexts. They also give students opportunities to develop and demonstrate Habits of Character.

Effective lesson planning begins with crafting clear standards-based learning targets in student-friendly language. Teachers plan strategies that ignite student curiosity and track student understanding, and they maximize opportunities for student voice, critical thinking, and leadership. Thoughtful lesson design leads students to want to learn, to work collaboratively, and to be aware of their learning process.

A. Designing the Lesson

1. Teachers craft high-quality learning targets in student-friendly language that reflects teachers' knowledge of their standards and their students. (See also *Core Practice 28: Crafting and Using Learning Targets.*)

2. Teachers vary the lesson formats they use. They make strategic decisions about format based on the learning targets and the needs of students.

3. Teachers craft lessons that set a clear purpose and ensure challenge. Teachers plan for challenge by asking the following questions of themselves:

   a. Based on required standards, what knowledge, skills, or habits do I most want my students to learn?

   b. How challenging are the texts I'm asking students to read relative to grade-level standards? How challenging are the tasks I'm asking them to do? What level of thinking (e.g., remembering, analyzing, creating) is required for this work?

   c. Am I giving students an opportunity to grapple? Am I making space for uncertainty and creative problem-solving?

   d. What questions should I ask? What is the purpose of each question?

4. Teachers scaffold instruction in the body of lessons to maximize student participation and discourse so that teachers talk less and students talk and think more. Teachers plan for engagement by asking the following questions of themselves:

   a. What will cause students to be curious and want to learn?

   b. How will I provide students with a vision of the learning target(s) in a way that gives them ownership of their learning?

   c. What lesson format will engage students in the day's key learning? What protocol or prompt will push students to ask questions of each other and encourage discussion?

   d. What do students already know? What sequenced steps will help them build new knowledge and skills?

   e. What framing question or task can I provide to connect students to an authentic personal, disciplinary, or social issue to engage and deepen their thinking?

   f. How will I differentiate for the needs of my diverse learners so that all are effectively supported and appropriately challenged?

5. Throughout the lesson and especially as it concludes, teachers help students to synthesize their current understanding and reflect on their progress so that students retain skills and concepts beyond an individual lesson or unit. Teachers plan for empowerment by asking the following questions of themselves:

   a. How will I structure the lesson so that students take responsibility for their learning? How will they assess and track their progress? How will we debrief learning experiences?

   b. How will students know what quality looks like, and how will I support them in producing high-quality work?

   c. Are there parts of the lesson that I can turn over to students to lead?

   d. Does the lesson give students an opportunity to articulate why the learning matters and how they might use it in new contexts?

   e. How will I help students capture key concepts so that they can remember them beyond the lesson?

B. Choosing a Lesson Format

1. Teachers choose a **Workshop 1.0 lesson format** when students have minimal background knowledge of the skill or content, or when first establishing classroom norms and building student confidence in learning strategies. Workshop 1.0 is a traditional "gradual release" lesson format, with the teacher modeling a skill and leading guided practice before students work on their own. Workshop 1.0 includes the following sequence of components:

   a. *Introduction*: The introduction taps into students' curiosity, sets a positive tone, builds the need to know, and links to previous learning. The learning target is shared during the introduction.

   b. *Mini lesson*: The mini lesson shows students how to meet the learning target through direct instruction. The teacher prepares students for success during practice by providing an explicit model of proficiency. The mini lesson may include modeling, think-aloud, demonstration, or mini lecture.

   c. *Guided practice*: Guided practice allows the teacher to assess student readiness for working independently by providing an opportunity for all students to try what was modeled with ample support. The teacher renames steps and addresses misconceptions.

   d. *Independent practice*: During independent practice, students practice what was modeled independently of the teacher. Teachers facilitate student thinking and understanding by asking probing questions and assess students' proficiency in relation to the learning target.

   e. *Sharing*: Teachers invite students to share work and ideas that show progress toward the learning target. Students and teachers celebrate successes.

   f. *Debrief*: Teachers invite students to create meaning by debriefing the lesson. Students think about the learning process and name how the lesson furthered their learning. Students and teachers assess proficiency toward the learning target and identify next steps.

2. Teachers choose a **Workshop 2.0 lesson format** when students are ready for more individual grappling with text and problems and less teacher modeling and guided practice. Workshop 2.0 is a revision of the traditional workshop model designed to address the demands of more rigorous standards. Workshop 2.0 includes the following sequence of components:

   a. *Engage*: Teachers engage students with a question, quote, object, picture, or problem that spurs thinking and invites them into the lesson's purpose or topic.

   b. *Grapple*: Teachers invite students to grapple independently with a complex text or problem. In early grades, this may be listening to a text that is read aloud.

   c. *Discuss*: Teachers provide a structured protocol that enables students to discuss, collaborate, and critique their interpretations or solutions for the problem or text.

   d. *Focus*: The teacher presents the learning target and a mini lesson or guided practice that introduces new concepts or skills, "mops up" misconceptions, or refocuses students' learning.

   e. *Apply*: Teachers ask students to apply their learning to a task that provides an opportunity to meet the learning target. During this section, the task may be differentiated, providing guided instruction for some students, but the text and target remain the same for all.

   f. *Synthesis*: Teachers invite students to debrief what they learned, share their reflection about how they learned, and assess their progress toward the learning target.

3. Teachers choose a **Discovery-Based lesson format** when they wish to prioritize exploration of new concepts or materials and to build curiosity and creative thinking. Teachers start a discovery-based lesson, such as the 5E's, with a provocative experience or problem that will help students to understand a broad concept within a discipline. They invite students to grapple with the problem in their own way, and then build skills, vocabulary, and conceptual understanding on a "need to know" basis. Learning targets are shared, or co-constructed with students, after exploration, discovery, and discussion. The components of a typical discovery-based lesson—the 5E's—follow:

   a. *Engage*: Teachers engage students (e.g., with a demonstration, brainstorm, problem) to raise questions and elicit responses that uncover what students know or think about the topic.

   b. *Explore*: Students then explore the topic together, without direct instruction from the teacher. The teacher asks probing questions of students and listens as they make meaning.

   c. *Explain*: Teachers ask students to explain their thinking based on their explorations and provide students with clarifications, definitions, and direct instruction.

   d. *Extend*: Students extend their knowledge of the topic by applying concepts and skills to new problems and tasks.

   e. *Evaluate*: Teachers assess students' knowledge or skills and ask them to assess their own learning.

4. Teachers choose **Protocol-Based lessons** when they wish to support students to discuss, collaborate, consult, share, critique, and present more productively and effectively.

Questions to consider when planning protocol-based lessons include:

a. What materials are needed to support the protocols (e.g., discussion role cards, peer critique response forms)?

b. Will the protocol last the entire lesson or support just one segment of the lesson? A lesson-length protocol structures an entire class period for a particular purpose. A Building Background Knowledge Workshop (BBK), a Socratic Seminar, and the Peer Critique protocol are examples of lesson-length protocols. Brief protocols such as Say Something, Turn and Talk, or Numbered Heads Together can be used to structure conversation and collaboration during one segment of a lesson.

5. Teachers choose **other lesson formats**—lecture, video, work sessions, labs, games—for specific purposes. Teachers embed engagement strategies to make the format more active when using lectures, video screenings, work sessions, and labs (e.g., using graphic organizers, mid-session questioning or critique, and Pair-Shares).

a. When students are learning content or practicing and mastering foundational facts, video, lectures, or memorization games may be appropriate.

b. When students are applying knowledge and skills to tasks, products, or performances, extended work sessions and labs may best serve the purpose.

Core Practice 11
Delivering Effective Lessons

In the EL Education model, teachers engage students in meaningful and productive work throughout the class period. When delivering lessons, teachers create purpose and build curiosity for students. They use classroom management techniques that promote equity and create a respectful, active, collaborative, and growth-oriented culture. They make time to confer with students and are aware of each student's level of understanding and participation. Teachers use practices that ensure all students grapple with challenging content. Teachers foster character by building positive relationships with students and inspiring each student to develop craftsmanship, perseverance, collaborative skills, and responsibility for learning. They promote critical thinking by asking that students make connections, perceive patterns and relationships, understand diverse perspectives, supply evidence for inferences and conclusions, and generalize to the big ideas of the discipline studied.

A. Starting with a Challenge and Setting Purpose

1. Teachers engage students with a task that invites them to grapple with the text or problem of the lesson. They use questions, graphics, video, artifacts, or hands-on experiences to connect students to the big idea or concept addressed in the lesson.

2. Teachers verbalize how new ideas and content build on prior instruction or students' prior knowledge.

3. Teachers strategically share learning targets with students during the focus section of a Workshop 2.0 lesson, or after a "hook," mystery experience, or discovery period.

4. Teachers pose strategic and open-ended questions that build students' curiosity and elicit multiple responses and perspectives from students.

5. Teachers describe next steps in the learning to orient students in the project or series of lessons and to provide the big picture for their learning.

B. Managing Students in the Active Classroom

1. Teachers develop and teach routines that maximize instructional time and student responsibility for effective lessons.

   a. Teachers streamline tasks that are non-instructional (e.g., taking attendance).

   b. Teachers establish routines for dealing with lesson interruptions such as visitors, announcements, and transitions. Students are able to refocus quickly.

   c. Teachers have routines for managing materials, furniture, and space. Students become adept at organizing the classroom for varied types of lessons and purposes.

   d. Teachers use specific and respectful techniques or signals for quickly getting and maintaining students' attention (e.g., call and response, raised hands, rhythmic clapping).

   e. Teachers introduce a brand-new skill or routine using demonstrations, think-alouds, role-plays, or Fishbowls to show what meeting the learning target looks like, for both academic learning targets and character learning targets.

   f. Teachers provide an instructional task (e.g., "do now" posted on the board) for when students enter the classroom or at the beginning of a lesson. Students always know what to do when they enter the room for a lesson.

2. Teachers use strategies to ensure that all students participate and embrace individual accountability.

   a. Teachers group students intentionally with the purpose of the activity in mind—for independent work, paired work, or larger groups. Groups are sometimes heterogeneous and sometimes homogeneous, depending on the purpose (e.g., students with different strengths and jobs working collaboratively on a problem; students with similar interests working collaboratively on a product; students working on the same phonetic or mathematical concept).

   b. Teachers provide or teach students to create graphic organizers, journals, concept maps, or other note-catchers that enable every student to record and represent thinking.

   c. Teachers create and post anchor charts, word walls, and other forms of "public notes" to synthesize student understanding and to provide students with a reference for future learning.

3. Teachers use protocols that model and encourage all students to participate respectfully in classroom discourse, take responsibility for their own learning, and contribute to the collective understanding of the group. Protocols

Delivering Effective Lessons (continued)

are procedures for discussion, collaboration, consultation, sharing, critique, and presenting that make classroom discourse more productive and effective. When using protocols, teachers implement the following strategies:

a. Explicitly teaching, rehearsing, and monitoring the steps of a selected protocol when it is first introduced

b. Using protocols in daily lessons when students are analyzing and discussing text, collaborating to solve problems, or critiquing each other's work

c. Using protocols to facilitate classroom meetings and Crews

d. Supporting students to reflect on how effective the protocol was and to revise and improve their use of the procedure

C. Supporting All Students[1]

1. Teachers gather detailed information about students' learning backgrounds, strengths, challenges, readiness, and interests.

2. Teachers pre-assess and/or ask students to self-assess against learning targets in order to determine flexible student groups and to provide all students with respectful tasks that will move them toward proficiency.

3. Teachers explicitly and intentionally teach academic and domain-specific vocabulary.

4. Teachers explicitly and intentionally teach background knowledge to fill in the gaps for students with less exposure to select topics.

5. Teachers scaffold instruction and tier assignments to support, challenge, and empower a variety of learners.

a. Teachers provide appropriate scaffolding during lessons (e.g., chunked text, annotated graphic organizers, guided practice).

b. Teachers provide more complex (not just more) tasks for advanced learners (e.g., supplementary text, extension problems).

D. Empowering Students through Reflection and Student-Engaged Assessment[2]

1. Teachers intentionally build a culture of collaboration, trust, and growth in which students feel that they belong and are respected. (See also *Core Practice 21: Creating a Community of Learning.*)

2. Teachers check for student understanding throughout lessons to ensure that every student demonstrates progress toward learning targets.

3. Teachers make time at the end of the lesson to debrief with students. They use varied structures to help students synthesize their current understanding and reflect on their progress so that students retain skills and concepts beyond an individual lesson or unit.

a. Teachers invite students to identify the thinking and problem-solving strategies they use during a lesson.

b. Teachers ask students to reflect on how their thinking has changed over time.

c. Teachers invite students to set goals for future learning and apply their learning to new contexts.

4. Teachers track students' progress toward mastery of learning targets regularly by using exit tickets, strategic observation, clickers, or other checks for understanding.

5. Teachers confer with students individually and in small groups to monitor each student's level of understanding and identify class-wide patterns.

6. Teachers provide structures (e.g., data trackers, portfolios) that teach students how to reflect on their own learning and collect evidence of growth.

7. Teachers keep observational and anecdotal records during student work sessions and when conferring with students and use them to inform next steps in instruction.

8. Teachers support students to lead their own learning by setting goals, analyzing data, and tracking their own progress (e.g., graphing their own reading fluency, analyzing patterns of error on a math test).

9. Teachers strategically administer on-demand assessments that accurately measure students' mastery of learning targets.

1. See also *Core Practice 19: Differentiating Instruction*
2. See also *Core Practice 29: Checking for Understanding in Daily Instruction*

Core Practice 12

Planning for and Supporting High-Quality Student Work

The EL Education model compels students to produce high-quality work that demonstrates complexity, craftsmanship, and authenticity. Teachers plan deeply to support students in creating products that demonstrate these qualities. They support students to create products for audiences beyond teachers and parents (e.g., a whole-class scientific study of a local pond, resulting in a water-quality report for the city board of health). Creating real work for real audiences motivates students to meet standards and engage in revision. In the process, they develop perseverance and realize that they can do more than they thought possible.

To create a culture of excellence, teachers have high expectations for all students and support all students with the scaffolding and equitable opportunities they need to achieve excellence. Students analyze models of excellence—student work and professional work—and use those models to build criteria for excellence in that genre of work. They receive targeted feedback from teachers, experts, and peers based on established criteria and revise their work through multiple drafts.

Teachers and school leaders analyze student work samples, task descriptors, and rubrics in professional learning to develop a common understanding of how to build complex, engaging tasks and how to support students to achieve high-quality work and meet standards.

A. Planning for Complexity in Student Work

1. Teachers design tasks that ask all students to do higher order, complex thinking. When creating the assignment, they consider the following questions:

   a. Does it connect to the big concepts that undergird my discipline or unite disciplines?

   b. Does it prioritize transfer of understanding to new contexts?

   c. Does it prioritize consideration of multiple perspectives?

   d. Does it require strong literacy skills, such as analyzing complex text and using text-based evidence to support writing or speaking?

   e. Does it require higher-order thinking skills like applying, analyzing, evaluating, and creating?

2. Teachers scaffold lessons to give all students practice in succeeding at higher-order thinking and decision-making. Scaffolding strategies include the following:

   a. Differentiating assignments to allow for student choice, interest, and innovation

   b. Considering the background knowledge, perspectives, resources, and home support of all students to make product creation accessible and equitable for all students

   c. Requiring students to do the planning and decision-

making that allow them to apply knowledge and skills in a new way

B. Planning for Craftsmanship in Student Work

1. Teachers plan backward from their vision of the product to identify supports students will need to create work that is accurate, detailed, and beautiful. With consideration for time and resources, their planning includes the following steps:

   a. Whenever possible, "test-driving" the product by creating their own in order to determine where students may struggle or need additional supports

   b. Identifying models of the product that can be used for critique lessons with students

   c. Identifying and acquiring professional tools and materials that enable students to master the conventions of the medium

   d. Sequencing skill lessons that enable students to learn and practice techniques required to create a high-quality product

   e. Identifying and contacting experts from within or outside the school who can share their wisdom, techniques, and the vocabulary of their field

   f. Sequencing lessons and scheduling adequate time for students to revise and polish their work multiple times in response to feedback

C. Planning for Authenticity in Student Work

1. Teachers plan backward from their vision of a product to ensure that it feels authentic to students and has meaning in the larger community. With consideration for time and resources, their planning includes the following steps:

   a. Choosing products that use work formats and standards from the professional world, rather than artificial school formats (e.g., students create a book review for a local newspaper instead of a book report for the teacher)

   b. Choosing products that connect academic standards with real-world issues, controversies, and local people and places

   c. Identifying or working with students to identify an audience beyond the teacher

   d. Building into the assignment opportunities for choice based on interest or learning style

   e. Identifying opportunities—collaboration with experts, fieldwork, or service experiences—that can enhance the authenticity of the product

   f. Prioritizing the original thinking of students—authentic personal voice and ideas, rather than memorized content or filling in blanks

   g. Looking for ways to motivate students with products that are also acts of service (e.g., creating informative signage for a local stream restoration project)

D. Developing a Culture of Excellence

1. Teachers create a classroom climate where students are excited about the opportunity and challenge of work, feel accountable to the group for deadlines, and demonstrate ownership of and pride in the work they create. (See also *Core Practice 22: Fostering Habits of Character.*)

2. Teachers create a culture of meaningful reflection and self-assessment by regularly engaging students in critiquing models or exemplars (either professional or student-created) and giving and receiving feedback on their own and peers' work. They establish norms that keep both formal and informal feedback emotionally safe, respectful, and always kind, specific, and helpful.

3. Teachers collect compelling models of work from students within and beyond the school and from the professional world. They display them to inspire high standards.

4. Teachers and school leaders regularly examine student work samples in grade-level teams, disciplinary teams, or whole-school professional learning to assess student understanding and skills. They assess assignments for their alignment to standards, complexity, authenticity, and high degree of craftsmanship. They identify strategies to support all students in achieving high-quality work.

E. Using Models, Critique, and Descriptive Feedback to Produce High-Quality Work

1. Teachers often structure lessons as whole-class critique sessions.

2. Teachers and students examine models of student work or professional work in order to name what quality looks like and identify strategies for improving quality.

   a. Teachers seek out inspiring and compelling models in the chosen genre so that students are excited to begin their own work.

   b. Teachers generate criteria lists with students and use them to construct task descriptors and rubrics. For example, instead of telling students what makes a good essay, students together critique essays of varying quality and create a list of qualities of a good essay.

   c. Teachers curate an archive of models, particularly in genres frequently used by students (e.g., lab reports, math word problem solutions).

3. Teachers demonstrate and teach protocols that support students in giving feedback to their peers. Teaching students to give and receive feedback includes the following:

   a. Modeling what giving and receiving quality feedback looks like and sounds like

   b. Developing specific questions to guide the protocol so that students focus on select aspects of the work (e.g., organization, detail)

   c. Using the same protocol multiple times and debriefing the process each time to build students' skills in giving and receiving kind, specific, and helpful feedback

4. Teachers sometimes invite guest experts to visit the classroom to give feedback on student work. Teachers prepare experts to focus on specific learning targets, model the classroom/school norms for communication, and build vocabulary and standards of the profession.

5. Teachers confer with students to provide descriptive feedback or comment on student work in writing during drafting and revision. This feedback *for learning* does not serve as an evaluative score or grade.

6. Teachers provide descriptive feedback that:

   a. Directs attention to the intended learning

   b. Is timely, ensuring that there is time for students to act on the feedback prior to summative assessment

   c. Addresses targeted misunderstandings and provides focused suggestions that students can act on

   d. Prompts students to think rather than simply make corrections

7. Teachers support students in analyzing their own thinking, writing, and creative process so that they can identify next steps for revision that refer back to agreed-upon criteria and move the work toward mastering learning targets.

8. Teachers require students to revise work intended for a public audience multiple times with the aim of meeting or exceeding the rubric criteria and achieving high quality (complexity, craftsmanship, and authenticity).

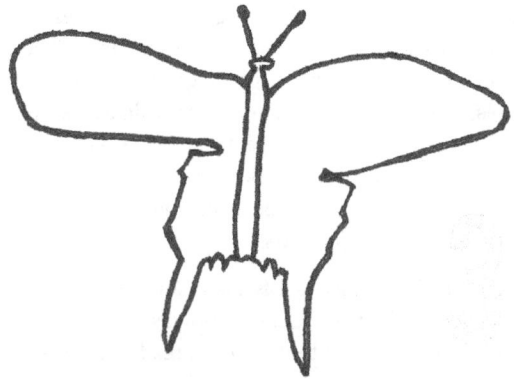

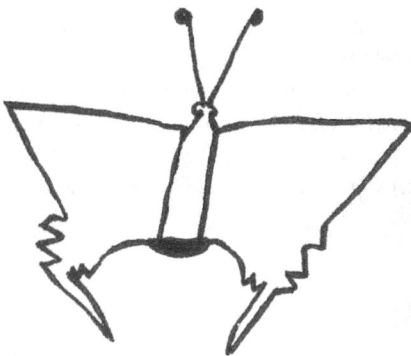

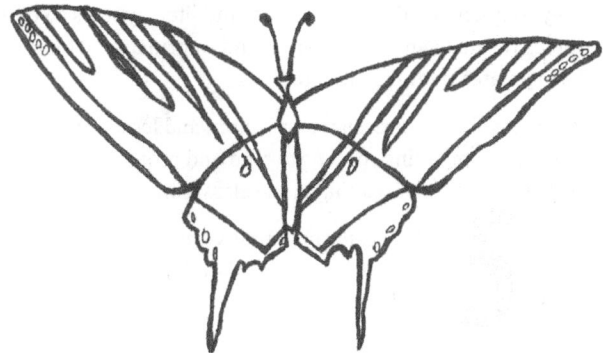

Teaching Reading across the Disciplines

In the EL Education model, teachers in all subjects and grade levels teach reading so that students build knowledge of the world and make sense of content by reading, thinking, talking, and writing about compelling topics. Teachers also provide many opportunities for students to read for joy, to satisfy innate curiosity, to revel in the pleasure of creative language, and to be transformed by interaction with other readers and writers.

Teachers challenge students to collaboratively and independently grapple with complex informational and literary texts. Teachers differentiate lessons to enable all students to comprehend a variety of grade-level texts, including primary sources, informational articles, literature, poetry, data sets, and real-world texts like speeches and informational graphics.

Teachers also provide texts at students' independent reading level, both for group or independent research (on the class topic of study) and for pleasure (on any topic of their choice). Teachers immerse students in reading for understanding and in lessons that require thinking, talking, and writing about text so that students develop the habit of supporting their claims with evidence when they speak and write. Content area teachers support students to read the formats and types of texts typical of their content (e.g., science articles, data sets) and to use domain-specific as well as academic vocabulary.

Across the grade levels, teachers focus on age-appropriate reading skills. For example, in primary grades, teachers balance content-based literacy and structured phonics lessons. At the secondary level, teachers of mathematics, science, history, technology, and the arts explicitly teach and support students to be strong readers of text within their discipline.

A. Planning for Reading Instruction

1. Teachers plan literacy-rich projects, case studies, and learning expeditions around compelling topics. They select a variety of texts—different genres, formats, reading levels, primary and secondary sources, data sets, and texts representing diverse perspectives on a topic—to teach content and develop skills. Teachers choose texts strategically to help students make meaning about a topic addressed in multiple texts.

2. Teachers of all subject areas and in all grade levels prioritize reading and text selection as part of the planning process. They ensure that students read a balance of informational and literary text. In language arts and humanities classes, as well as interdisciplinary studies, they frequently pair informational and literary texts so that topics resonate and both literary and informational texts have greater relevance for students.

3. Teachers choose or design curriculum and lessons that give students compelling reasons to read and promote a need-to-know culture of reading in the classroom.

4. Teachers evaluate text for quantitative and qualitative measures of complexity as part of planning lessons and longer units of study.

5. For close reading, teachers ensure that all students have access to grade-level complex text. They may differentiate the length of text and the tasks required of students to access the text but avoid differentiating the texts themselves. When students are reading independently for research or pleasure, teachers provide varied texts so that students at all levels read texts that they can comprehend independently. (See also *Core Practice 19: Differentiating Instruction*.)

6. Teachers select protocols and lesson formats (e.g., Workshop 2.0) that encourage students to process text through thinking, talking, and writing.

7. Teachers plan text-dependent questions in advance based on their larger teaching purpose: both the content understanding they want students to develop and the grade-level literacy standards students need to master. Their questions require students to search for explicit and implicit evidence to support their thinking. Teachers include questions that require higher-order thinking (e.g., analysis, evaluation), not just fact-finding.

B. Supporting All Students to Succeed as Readers[3]

1. Teachers in all subject areas and at all grade levels teach reading to acquire content and to develop skills such as analyzing, evaluating, researching, and writing.

2. In primary grades, teachers balance content-based literacy and structured phonics lessons.

   a. Teachers conduct close read-alouds of content-rich texts using listening and sharing protocols that support students in analyzing and discussing complex text.

   b. Teachers build students' foundational skills by intentionally using texts that support students to understand how language works. Foundational skills include:

      i. Concepts of print

      ii. Phonemic awareness

      iii. Word recognition

      iv. Fluency

      v. Basic conventions of spoken and written English

   c. Teachers make time for active literacy blocks that encourage young readers to play and create with language, explore new skills, read books they choose and can read at an independent level, and practice skills and Habits of Character.

3. In content areas and secondary classes, teachers give special attention to the research standards at their grade level.

   a. Teachers engage students in rich and rigorous evidence-based conversations about the texts they use for their research.

   b. Teachers require students to use the information and evidence they collect in research to support their ideas and arguments in speaking and writing.

4. All teachers regularly facilitate close reading lessons, in which students read and reread short complex texts to uncover layers of meaning and consider author's craft. In primary grades, teachers do this through close read-alouds.

5. Teachers require students to grapple with complex texts as independently as possible; teachers model to clarify and reteach after students have tried on their own.

6. Teachers require students to code or annotate text, refer to the text to answer questions, discuss using evidence from the text, and write to demonstrate their understanding.

7. Teachers use protocols (e.g., Socratic Seminar, Conversation Cafe, Say Something) to structure students' discussion of text, engage all students, and hold them accountable for respectful and productive conversation.

8. Teachers provide tools (graphic organizers, anchor charts, reading response journals, word walls) that enable students to record text-based evidence, document their thinking, and reference vocabulary.

9. Teachers use common language, grounded in the language of the standards, to teach reading (e.g., citing evidence, inferring, identifying main ideas) and habits that support successful reading (rereading, annotating).

10. Teachers explicitly teach students to analyze texts for both meaning and author's craft.

11. Teachers teach vocabulary both implicitly (by immersing students in rich language) and explicitly. They focus lessons intensely on word-learning strategies (e.g., using context clues, affixes, reference materials) to build students' ability to acquire more words independently.

C. Creating a Culture of Reading

1. Teachers present themselves as readers and model appreciation and enjoyment of written text. Adults in the school and larger community read with students and discuss their own reading habits and passions.

2. Teachers frame complex text as an exciting challenge that rewards readers with a sense of achievement and pride, an adventure that demands courage, perseverance, and learnable skills. Teachers encourage students to take academic risks in their reading and provide multiple low-stakes opportunities to learn from mistakes. (See also *Core Practice 22: Fostering Habits of Character.*)

3. Teachers provide opportunities for students to read every day, throughout the day, for a variety of purposes and to discuss and write about what they read. Teachers encourage students to share verbally, to listen respectfully to other readers, and to value multiple perspectives.

4. Teachers celebrate vocabulary, both general academic and domain-specific vocabulary, across the school in lessons, Crew, and displays.

5. Teachers model and verbalize that reading can be joyful and interesting. They set up structures for accountable, independent reading that promote reading as a way to learn about the world and connect with other readers and writers.

---

3. See also *Core Practice 19: Differentiating Instruction.*

Teaching Reading across the Disciplines (continued)

6. Teachers incorporate readings of quotes, short stories, poems, and other short texts into Crew and other schoolwide structures, such as community meetings, to underscore the importance of literacy.

7. Teachers know their students as readers and help students find texts that match individual needs and interests, are accessible and engaging, and that help students build deep knowledge about the world around them.

8. Teachers create classrooms that are print-rich environments with classroom libraries and digital resources that include a variety of sources in multiple genres, representing differing perspectives and a variety of reading levels.

9. Students can articulate the value of reading in their lives and in the world. They read with curiosity, wonder, and joy.

10. Students develop the habits of building strong content knowledge, comprehending as well as critiquing, valuing evidence, and understanding multiple perspectives and cultures.

D. Assessing Reading[4]

1. Teachers provide recording forms, graphic organizers, or reading response journals. Students document their understanding and thinking and provide evidence of growth over time.

2. Teachers regularly confer with students about the content of their reading to deepen students' thinking about their reading, reflect on their growth as readers, and help them set and track goals.

3. Teachers assess student understanding of text through text-dependent questions with verbal or short written responses. Whether oral or written, such questions require students to substantiate their claims and interpretations with evidence from the text.

4. Teachers craft assessments to determine students' level of standards-aligned reading proficiency. In the primary grades, teachers regularly assess students' progress through observation, running records, or age-appropriate literacy assessments.

5. Teachers use diagnostic and normed interim assessment data to identify areas for growth and inform reading instruction. Teaching teams meet regularly to discuss concerns arising from data.

6. Teachers share data with students and support them in analyzing their own data and setting goals for improvement in reading.

---

4. See also *Core Practice 29: Checking for Understanding in Daily Instruction* and *Core Practice 30: Using Assessments to Boost Student Achievement*

Core Practice 14

Teaching Writing across the Disciplines

In the EL Education model, writing is taught across the curriculum in K–12 classrooms. Teachers provide many opportunities for students to write for multiple purposes: to express their thoughts and feelings, to tell stories, to demonstrate understanding, to reflect on learning, to communicate ideas, and to develop and polish the craft of writing. Students write to learn (as a way of putting their emerging thinking on paper). They also learn to write, revise, and polish authentic pieces in varied genres for audiences beyond the teacher. Teachers develop and teach a common language for the process of writing and the elements of good writing. They use consistent practices for teaching and assessing writing.

At the secondary level, teachers of mathematics, science, history, technology, and the arts explicitly teach and support quality writing within their discipline. Teachers provide opportunities for students to write like historians, scientists, mathematicians, and artists. While the nature and amount of writing varies by discipline and grade level, writing is a central vehicle for learning and communicating in all classrooms.

A. Planning for Writing Instruction

1. Teachers design writing tasks that address standards-aligned learning targets. In the course of the school year, tasks encompass a variety of writing genres and formats (e.g., arguments or opinion pieces supported by evidence, research-based informational writing, narratives, poetry, personal essays).

2. Teachers plan writing tasks that support learning throughout a project, case study, or learning expedition so that students build knowledge and can create a final product with deep understanding about their topic. Teachers create graphic organizers, journals, or other note-catchers to accompany reading lessons. Teachers create on-demand written response tasks to assess students' knowledge and writing skills prior to completing a final product.

3. Teachers identify authentic audiences within and beyond the school community for whom students can write. They design writing tasks for products that will be revised and polished over many weeks and that mirror formats or genres used in the professional world (e.g., brochures, letters, books, how-to manuals, advertisements).

4. Teachers are aware of the writing formats commonly used in different disciplines (e.g., scientific journals, oral histories, mathematical solutions that explain process). They collect and archive exemplars of high-quality student writing in formats used commonly in their classrooms to use as models for class critique lessons and can explain what quality writing looks like in multiple contexts.

5. Teachers craft thoughtfully scaffolded writing lessons to support all learners in a variety of writing tasks and with a particular writing task. They design anchor charts, writing process trackers, rubrics, and other tools to scaffold the writing process for students.

6. Teachers work to include diverse authors who expose students to a variety of cultures and voices when choosing professionally written models for students to learn from and emulate.

B. Supporting All Students to Write Effectively

1. Teachers ensure that students have multiple opportunities to discuss and rethink their ideas before and during a writing task.

2. Teachers recognize speaking and listening as ways of processing and organizing ideas for writing.

3. Teachers encourage students to return to the text multiple times and challenge students to use accurate text-based evidence when writing for evidence-based tasks.

4. Teachers in all subject areas require students to write to learn.

   a. Teachers ask students to read, analyze, discuss, and write about texts in order to evaluate and synthesize evidence they will use in their writing.

   b. Teachers assign journals, synthesis statements, and other forms of written response in which students document their learning about the topic.

   c. Teachers require students to use information and evidence they collect through reading and research to support the ideas and arguments in authentic writing products.

5. Teachers in all subject areas require students to learn to write.

   a. Teachers explicitly teach the recursive process of writing, from building knowledge to prewriting, drafting, conferring, revising (for author's craft), editing (for conventions), and making the work public. They support students to understand that writers often go back and forth between these "steps" many times.

b. Students articulate and use the writing process to create high-quality work that is complex, well crafted, and authentic. In the primary grades, this means teachers support students with getting their words down on paper but are careful to honor students' word choice and organization of ideas. (See also *Core Practice 12: Planning for and Supporting High-Quality Student Work.*)

6. Students and teachers use a common language for the elements of writing (e.g., ideas, organization, style, sentence fluency, conventions) and the habits that support successful writing (e.g., perseverance, revising, critiquing, editing).

7. Teachers build understanding of the writing process and author's craft through structured critique lessons that feature student work as models whenever possible. These models are not used as examples of perfection, but rather they are analyzed together with students to build student-friendly criteria for quality that can be used to create rubrics and guide students. (See also *Core Practice 12: Planning for and Supporting High-Quality Student Work.*)

8. Teachers create anchor charts with students that document student understanding of the elements of quality writing and the writing process. They are displayed so that students can reference them while they are working toward quality writing.

9. Teachers focus on one skill or strategy at a time (e.g., crafting a thesis, proper citation style). They chunk specific standards, techniques, and elements of writing with targeted mini lessons.

10. In the content areas, teachers explicitly teach writing with attention to the vocabulary, writing formats, and style of their discipline (e.g., lab reports in science class, constructed responses in mathematics class).

11. Teachers explicitly teach the skills students need to compare, contrast, and apply information they gather from text, including analyzing an argument, summarizing information, and attributing quotes accurately.

12. Teachers explicitly teach students how to gather relevant information from multiple print and digital sources and how to evaluate sources for reliability, credibility, and accuracy.

13. Teachers provide feedback on drafts and revisions to individual students to improve students' writing and understanding of what quality looks like and sounds like in their own writing.

14. Teachers use peer critique protocols to teach students how to give and receive kind, specific, and helpful feedback on writing. Students use the rubric or criteria list to provide effective descriptive feedback.

15. Teachers provide contextualized, explicit grammar and conventions instruction tied to the demands of a specific writing task.

16. Teachers differentiate scaffolding for the writing process to support writers in making progress toward high-quality writing products. This may include using different graphic organizers, providing writing technology or tiered assignments, or other ways of differentiating for diverse writers' needs. (See also *Core Practice 19: Differentiating Instruction.*)

C. Creating a Culture of Writing

1. Teachers present themselves as writers and model appreciation and enjoyment of writing for communication and pleasure. Adults in the school and larger community are invited to write with students and to discuss their own writing habits and passions.

2. Teachers frame writing as an exciting challenge that rewards writers with a sense of achievement and pride, and as an adventure that demands courage, perseverance, and skill. Teachers encourage students to take academic risks in their writing and provide multiple low-stakes opportunities to learn from mistakes. (See also *Core Practice 22: Fostering Habits of Character.*)

3. Teachers create classroom environments where students can express their thinking, viewpoints, and creativity in writing. They encourage students to share what they write, to listen respectfully to other writers, and to value multiple perspectives.

4. Teachers and school leaders celebrate strong writing and strong growth in writing throughout the school by displaying and calling out exemplars of student writing.

5. Teachers raise students' awareness of an author's craft when reading across the disciplines. They teach students to read for author's craft and to write with the reader's expectations in mind.

6. Teachers know their students as writers and help them find writing models that match individual needs and interests and inspire students to try new techniques, styles, and formats.

7. Students can articulate the value of writing in their lives and in the world. They develop the habits of valuing evidence, responding to the demands of purpose and audience, using communication strategies

effectively, analyzing multiple perspectives, and writing independently.

D. Assessing Writing

1. Teachers regularly confer with students and encourage them to reflect on their own choices and strategies as authors. Students self-assess and revise based on feedback from teachers and peers. They can articulate how their revisions create more effective writing.

2. Teachers debrief writing workshops to deepen students' thinking about their writing process and encourage students to reflect on their own growth as writers.

3. Teachers assess written communication skills through short tasks (e.g., sentence or paragraph writing, outlines) and longer written assignments.

4. Teachers use classroom or school-based assessments and standardized state or national writing assessments to assess students' level of standards-aligned writing proficiency.

5. Teachers look closely at completed student work to assess students' ability to write for a variety of purposes, audiences, and genres.

6. Teachers use writing assessment data to identify areas for growth and to inform writing instruction. Teaching teams meet regularly to discuss concerns arising from data.

7. Teachers use rubrics based on standards and student-generated criteria to assess and provide feedback on writing during the process and to assess revised writing products.

8. Teachers and students document growth in writing over time, as well as students' reflections on that growth, in student portfolios.

Core Practice 15
Teaching Mathematics

In the EL Education model, mathematics is taught in stand-alone mathematics classes. Whenever possible, it is also integrated into other subjects, projects, case studies, and learning expeditions. Teachers in all disciplines and grade levels model mathematical passion and courage by addressing gaps in their own mathematical understanding, explicitly exploring the mathematical dimensions of their discipline and modeling mathematical thinking. Teachers support all students to think like mathematicians and cultivate mathematical habits of mind, including curiosity, risk-taking, perseverance, valuing evidence, precision, and craftsmanship. All students are prepared to engage in high-level mathematics classes, because such classes often function as gateways to access other classes and courses at the secondary level and in college. Mathematical thinking and learning is showcased and discussed throughout the building.

Teachers choose challenging curriculum and generative problems that will enable students to discover the mathematical concepts behind algorithms and procedures. They engage students by asking them to grapple with complex problems independently and to discuss and critique each other's strategies. Students learn to reason abstractly and quantitatively, to model real-world situations mathematically, and to construct and critique mathematical arguments. Teachers deepen students' conceptual understanding by equipping them to solve unfamiliar and complex problems. Deep conceptual understanding leads to mathematical fluency in which students are able to apply numeracy in various, more complex contexts. Teachers support students to build on foundational facts—vocabulary, algorithms, formulas, and number facts (such as times tables)—as one part of mathematical fluency. Students learn to use technology strategically in problem solving.

A. Planning for Mathematics Instruction

1. Teachers invest time and effort to collaboratively unpack mathematics standards both vertically and horizontally, prioritize and cluster them, and match the mathematical concepts in the standards to challenging and, often, real-world problems.

2. Teachers choose problems that invite multiple problem-solving strategies, representations, and/or solutions and that generate understanding of key mathematical concepts.

3. Teachers test-drive problems to analyze how students might solve them and to anticipate misconceptions and opportunities for instruction.

4. Teachers preplan questions aligned to problems and tasks to promote student discourse of key ideas.

5. Teachers craft learning targets that focus on the key mathematical concept or skill of the lesson in student-friendly language. (See also *Core Practice 28: Crafting and Using Learning Targets*.)

6. Teachers identify both formative and summative assessments that measure progress toward learning targets. These may include class work, math journals, mathematics discussions, and exit tickets in addition to traditional exams and quizzes.

7. Teachers design lessons that require students to grapple independently and collaboratively, participate in mathematical discourse, apply mathematical concepts, and synthesize their learning to connect new understandings to the broader field of mathematics.

B. Teaching Conceptual Understanding

1. Teachers invite students to discover big mathematical ideas by grappling with and solving problems. They use purposeful questions to assess and advance students' reasoning about ideas.. This builds mathematical courage, creativity, and confidence.

2. Teachers often begin a lesson with a problem or problem set that inspires inquiry and encourages grappling. Students return to the grapple problem throughout the class period or over more than one class period.

3. Teachers use lessons structures and routines, such as Workshop 2.0, that allow students to spend the majority of class time applying their learning and developing conceptual understanding. (See also *Core Practice 11: Delivering Effective Lessons*.)

4. Teachers animate standard curricula and resources with engaging, real-world examples and rich tasks with multiple entry points. They use mathematical modeling to connect mathematics to other disciplines. Students and teachers use diagrams, manipulatives, and models to support the translation from concrete to abstract representations and vice versa.

5. Teachers foster rich mathematical discourse in the classroom by asking open-ended questions, showcasing students' own thinking and arguments about mathematics, and teaching the vocabulary of the discipline.

6. Teachers model multiple ways of explaining mathematical thinking verbally, symbolically, graphically, and in writing.

7. Teachers provide protocols that allow students to present and critique their own mathematical arguments and those of others.

8. Teachers use a "neutral" response when students are giving answers or explaining their thinking (e.g., "Is that correct?" "Does that make sense?"). This encourages other students to do their own evaluation independent of the teacher.

9. Teachers identify misconceptions and monitor students' work in progress via strategic questions designed to guide students' thinking so that they ultimately arrive at precise and deep understanding.

C. Teaching Foundational Mathematics

1. Teachers build excitement and motivation for students to acquire foundational facts by using the following strategies:

   a. Helping students develop a belief in their own capacity and celebrating their growth in mastering facts

   b. Focusing on problem solving and conceptual understanding so that students develop a need-to-know attitude about foundational facts

   c. Providing many opportunities for students to practice specific foundational mathematics (e.g., number facts, algorithms, formulas, and vocabulary) required by standards so that students see how fluency empowers their mathematical thinking

   d. Using and discussing strategies and graphic representations that demonstrate patterns, relationships, and shortcuts

   e. Asking students to set goals related to learning targets for foundational mathematics and monitoring progress toward targets with individualized charts, interim assessments, and/or math journals

2. Teachers and leaders provide extended in-school opportunities, mathematics labs, small group interventions, and tutorials for students who need extra support in learning foundational mathematics skills.

3. Teachers teach students to strategically use technology tools, not as a substitute for learning foundational facts, but to enhance conceptual understanding and problem-solving dexterity.

D. Teaching Problem-Solving Skills

1. Teachers promote flexibility in mathematical thinking by celebrating diverse thinking and multiple-solution strategies.

   a. Students are supported to move from concrete to more abstract problem-solving strategies.

   b. Students have opportunities to problem-solve before being taught standard algorithms.

   c. Students explore alternative algorithms, strategies, and shortcuts with the goal of choosing the most efficient strategies for a specific context.

2. Teachers facilitate frequent class discussion and analysis of problem-solving approaches. They provide problem-solving frameworks that can be used to approach both familiar and unfamiliar problems.

3. Teachers regularly ask students to create as well as solve mathematical problems.

4. Teachers ask students to construct viable arguments for solutions and justify their reasoning with evidence including calculations, mathematical stories, graphs, and diagrams.

5. Teachers support students to be precise and craft accurate, efficient, and elegant mathematical solutions.

E. Creating a Culture of Mathematical Literacy

1. Teachers explore their own perceptions and mindsets regarding mathematics. They support each other's ongoing learning as mathematicians.

2. Teachers continually refresh and expand their own mathematical content knowledge, individually and collectively, through professional learning.

3. Teachers learn mathematics instructional techniques and discuss teaching strategies and interventions appropriate for specific student needs.

4. Teachers empower all students to see themselves as mathematicians, refuting stereotypes about who can succeed in mathematics and celebrating the past and current mathematical contributions of diverse individuals and groups.

5. Teachers emphasize the habits of mathematical thinking and create protocols and norms for mathematical discourse. They focus on growth mindset and reinforce students' mathematical courage to speak up in class, risk mistakes, explain their thinking, and persist in challenging problems.

6. Teachers celebrate the mathematical thinking and growth of students by displaying anchor charts and examples of student work to demonstrate students' mathematical literacy.

Teaching Mathematics (continued)

7. Teachers across content areas invite students to apply numeracy beyond mathematics class (e.g., learning expeditions or other core content areas, Crew, community meetings, service-learning work) to reinforce and develop foundational facts and number sense and to model mathematical application. Students are involved in mathematics every day in dedicated classes and outside of mathematics class.

F. Assessing Mathematics

1. Teachers and students use multiple methods for assessing mathematical understanding, such as observations, learning logs, math journals, portfolio reflections, and mathematical models built by students, as well as quizzes, tests, and performance assessments.

2. Teachers regularly and effectively use student-engaged assessment strategies during lessons. They ensure that all students have multiple opportunities to learn and demonstrate progress toward learning targets.

3. Teachers track mathematical discourse as one means of judging collective and individual student understanding.

4. Teachers debrief whole-class mathematical discourse to help students synthesize their mathematical thinking and reflect on their growth as mathematicians.

5. Teachers support students in regularly analyzing data from assessments to understand specific areas and general patterns of strength and weakness. (See also *Core Practice 29: Checking for Understanding in Daily Instruction.*)

6. Teachers regularly analyze data from student work and from formative and summative assessments to identify areas of need and inform instruction.

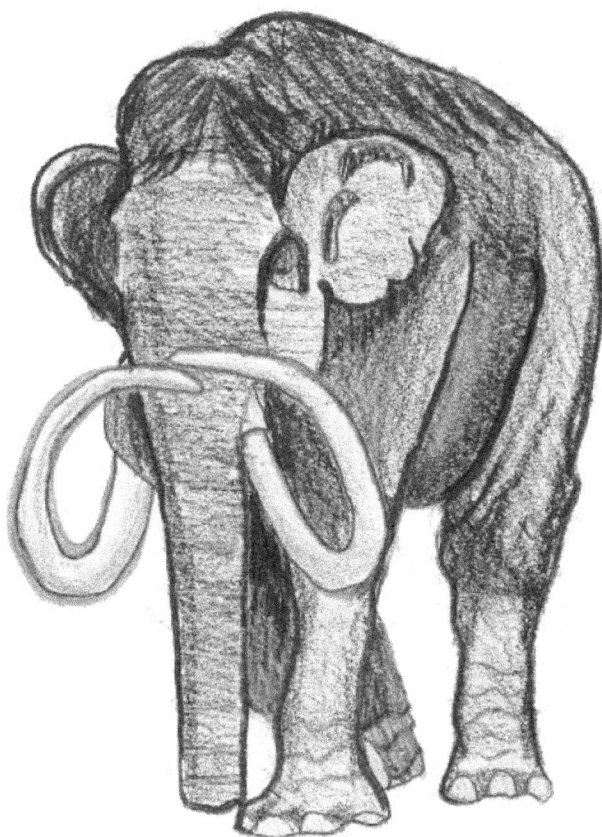

Teaching Science

In the EL Education model, teachers prioritize students' understanding of enduring science concepts so that they can apply that understanding to the modern world. Teachers view science as a way to develop students' capacity to interpret the natural world critically and to engage productively in it. Teachers support students to read, write, think, and work as scientists do. They use learning expeditions, case studies, projects, problem-based content, collaboration with professional scientists and engineers, and interactive instructional practices to foster inquiry and enable authentic student research. When possible, student research contributes to the school or broader community.

Teachers reinforce the connections among science, mathematics, engineering, and technology as they lift up enduring ideas that cut across these disciplines. They cultivate scientific thinking and disciplinary skills in close reading, questioning, experimenting, using data, and communicating scientifically. Students learn to be logical, accurate, insightful, and unbiased when supporting statements with reliable scientific evidence. In addition, because appreciation and stewardship of the natural world is part of the EL Education model, teachers address environmental literacy as part of the science curriculum at all levels.

A. Planning for Science Instruction

1. Teachers unpack and bundle science standards to focus on significant and enduring ideas that cut across science disciplines (e.g., cause and effect, systems and systems models, structure and function).

2. In collaboration with colleagues, teachers plan the year's science scope and sequence to "cover" the broad scope of topics required by standards—a survey approach—and also to "uncover" key concepts through a case study (or deep dive) approach (e.g., a case study of ants within a broader study of animal groups and classification). Long-term planning entails the following:

   a. Crafting standards-aligned learning targets for knowledge, skills, and scientific thinking (e.g., questioning)

   b. Creating engaging lessons that provide a broad overview (e.g., cellular structures in biology)

   c. Selecting case studies or narrow topics that illuminate enduring concepts (e.g., a local frog as a study of indicator species and ecosystem relationships)

3. Teachers choose scientific topics as the basis of learning expeditions, case studies, and projects at all grade levels. They identify controversial scientific issues or local connections that animate topics and have strong potential for original research.

4. Teachers design research opportunities and products that engage students in authentic research that contributes to their communities (e.g., kindergartners analyzing conditions for optimal growth in their school garden, high school students testing indoor air quality in the school to inform recommendations to the board of education).

5. Teachers structure opportunities for scientific inquiry that allow students to participate in scientific research and problem solving that approximate adult science, including framing questions, designing methods to answer questions or test hypotheses, determining appropriate timelines and costs, calibrating instruments, conducting trials, writing reports, and presenting and defending results.

6. Teachers select a variety of primary and secondary source materials to supplement or replace textbooks (e.g., trade books, peer-reviewed journal articles, government documents). These texts serve as both anchor texts to bolster students' conceptual understanding and mentor texts to model the structure and style of scientific writing.

7. Teachers supplement texts with rich experiences to support conceptual understanding, including labs, fieldwork, and interaction with experts.

8. Teachers design assessments for lessons that address content knowledge, scientific thinking, and integrity in applying the scientific method.

B. Teaching Scientific Concepts and Skills

1. Teachers use complex scientific text to build students' understanding of scientific content and teach scientific literacy skills through the following actions:

   a. Conducting close reading lessons of informational text (and sometimes fiction) that includes accurate scientific information

   b. Teaching students to comprehend multiple forms of scientific documents, including texts, maps, models, diagrams, charts, graphs, tables, and timelines

Teaching Science (continued)

c. Explicitly teaching domain-specific vocabulary related to the topic of study

2. Teachers engage students in complex, problem-based labs and investigations that require students to:

a. Ask testable scientific questions

b. Design and/or conduct experiments

c. Use the tools of science with accuracy, care, and expertise

d. Collect, represent, analyze, and report data

e. Interpret results and reflect on methodology

3. Teachers encourage rich scientific discourse in which students evaluate multiple perspectives on a topic, take and defend positions, and consider alternative viewpoints.

4. Teachers require students to construct arguments and make written and verbal claims supported by scientific evidence so that students practice:

a. Making logical assumptions

b. Collecting accurate data

c. Drawing insightful conclusions

d. Supporting statements with reliable and unbiased scientific evidence

5. Teachers ask students to represent and reflect on their thinking (e.g., develop science notebooks, create analogies, make graphs, create technical drawings, build models).

6. Teachers use both student work samples and professional models (e.g., reports, lab notebooks, informational books, scientific diagrams) to explicitly teach what quality writing in science looks like and sounds like.

7. Teachers sometimes incorporate service-learning projects connected to content.

C. Creating a Culture of Science Inquiry

1. Teachers empower all students to see themselves as scientists by refuting stereotypes about who can succeed in science and celebrating the past and current scientific contributions of diverse individuals and groups.

2. Teachers, students, and school leaders celebrate, display, and discuss the natural and physical world throughout the school.

3. Teachers support student appreciation and stewardship of the natural world through experiences, projects, and service learning.

4. Schools develop indoor and outdoor areas, such as science labs, computer labs, workshops, gardens, and natural areas, to stimulate students' interest in science and technology.

5. Teachers display student work that provides evidence of scientific research and learning in public areas of the school.

6. Teachers welcome curiosity, reward creativity, and encourage thoughtful scientific questioning. They make students' questions visible and create opportunities for students to pursue answers to their own questions.

D. Assessing Scientific Understanding

1. Teachers create opportunities for students to demonstrate their *understanding* (not memorization) of science concepts (e.g., evolutionary adaptation, Newton's laws of physics). Opportunities include explaining concepts accurately to others using graphic representations, models, demonstrations, writing, and peer teaching.

2. Teachers regularly check for understanding and misconceptions. They support students in tracking their own progress toward learning targets and provide feedback that helps students make progress.

3. Teachers debrief learning by inviting students to generalize and apply concepts and procedures to other contexts and problems. They encourage students to reflect on what they learned, how they learned it, and how they can transfer it to new contexts.

4. Teachers and students use multiple methods of assessing understanding, such as one-on-one discussions, observations, Science Talks, science notebooks, portfolio reflections, and student-constructed scientific models, as well as quizzes, tests, and performance assessments.

Core Practice 17
Teaching Social Studies

In the EL Education model, teachers of social studies prioritize students' understanding of enduring concepts so that they can apply that understanding to the modern world. Teachers view social studies as a way to develop students' capacity to interpret their world critically and to engage productively in it. Teachers support students to read, write, think, and work as social scientists do. They use learning expeditions, case studies, projects, problem-based content, collaborating with social science professionals, and interactive instructional practices to foster inquiry and enable authentic student research. When possible, student research contributes to the school community or broader community.

Teachers help students understand the big picture and timeline of history through survey-type lessons but emphasize historical frameworks, trends, and concepts rather than memorization of myriad facts and details. By focusing on big ideas, teachers support students to appreciate and understand diverse cultures and understand connections among ancient and modern cultures. Whenever possible, teachers choose strategic points to step out of survey mode and dive deep into case studies (often on local topics), during which students can engage in research and work as social scientists. Teachers also cultivate historical thinking and disciplinary skills such as close reading, questioning, using data, and communicating as social scientists do.

A. Planning for Social Studies Instruction

1. Teachers unpack and bundle social studies standards to emphasize the enduring themes—or big ideas—of social studies (e.g., the common elements of civilizations; the roles that governments play; the relationship among geography, industry, and culture).

2. In collaboration with colleagues, teachers plan the year's scope and sequence to "cover" the breadth of required standards and put particular events in a broader historical context (a survey approach) and also to "uncover" key concepts through a case study approach (diving deep). Planning entails the following:

   a. Crafting standards-aligned learning targets for knowledge, skills, and historical thinking (e.g., interpreting data)

   b. Creating engaging lessons that provide a broad overview of topics (e.g., surveys of time periods or geographical regions) using timelines and graphic representations to help students comprehend the big picture of historical relationships

   c. Selecting case studies or narrow topics that intertwine history, government, economics, geography, and culture,and illuminate enduring themes (e.g., a case study of Shays' Rebellion that allows students to develop an understanding of challenges in the founding of the United States, as well as the themes of power, authority, and governance)

3. Teachers choose social studies topics as the basis of learning expeditions, case studies, and projects at all grade levels. They identify engaging local issues that animate topics and have strong potential for original research (e.g., a case study of a local civil rights leader embedded in a study of the American civil rights movement).

4. Teachers design research opportunities and products that engage students in authentic research that contributes to their communities (e.g., third-graders writing and advocating for a school constitution; middle school students writing and publishing a book about local peace activists).

5. Teachers structure opportunities for students to do original research or problem solving using professionally recognized social science methods, including framing questions, designing methods to answer questions, determining appropriate timelines and costs, conducting surveys or interviews, writing reports or narratives, and presenting and defending ideas.

6. Teachers select a variety of primary and secondary source materials to supplement or replace textbooks (e.g., trade books, journal articles, government documents). These texts serve as both anchor texts to bolster students' conceptual understanding and mentor texts to model the structure and style of social science writing (e.g., an oral history or white paper).

7. Teachers supplement texts with rich experiences to support conceptual understanding, including visits to cultural sites, fieldwork, and interaction with experts.

8. Teachers design assessments that address content knowledge, historical thinking, and integrity in applying social science methods.

Teaching Social Studies (continued)

B. Teaching Social Studies Concepts and Skills

1. Teachers use complex text to build students' understanding of social studies content and teach literacy skills through the following actions:

   a. Conducting close reading lessons of informational text (and sometimes fiction) related to a social studies topic

   b. Teaching students to comprehend multiple forms of social science documents, including texts, maps, diagrams, charts, graphs, tables, and timelines

   c. Explicitly teaching domain-specific vocabulary related to the topic of study

2. Teachers use a survey approach to teach geography and the broad timelines of history that provide the big picture of social studies.

3. Teachers use a case study approach to dive deep and explore local and/or specific historical questions with depth and complexity.

4. Teachers engage students in complex, problem-based activities, such as investigations based on authentic questions, through the following actions:

   a. Teaching students to use methods approximating those used by professional social scientists (e.g., oral history, surveys, demographic data collection) with accuracy, care, and expertise at all levels

   b. Requiring students to collect, represent, analyze, and report real data as a part of inquiry

5. Teachers ask students to explore multiple perspectives when learning about a topic and to analyze and evaluate evidence for opposing views. This may include exploring the history and evolution of historical thinking, considering such questions as who records history and how is it interpreted.

6. Teachers require students to construct arguments and make verbal and written claims supported by evidence so that students practice:

   a. Making logical assumptions

   b. Drawing insightful conclusions

   c. Supporting claims with unbiased and reliable evidence

7. Teachers ask students to represent and reflect on their thinking (e.g., develop history notebooks, create analogies, make graphs, create technical drawings, build models).

8. Teachers use both student work samples and professional models (e.g., community ethnography, annotated maps, infographics) to explicitly teach what quality writing in social studies looks and sounds like.

9. Teachers sometimes incorporate service-learning projects connected to content.

C. Creating a Culture of Social Studies Inquiry

1. Teachers empower all students to see themselves as historians by refuting stereotypes about who records history and highlighting the past and current historical contributions of diverse individuals and groups.

2. Teachers, students, and school leaders celebrate, display, and discuss culture and society throughout the school. They address issues of diversity and equity that impact students and their communities.

3. Teachers support student appreciation and stewardship of their communities through experiences, projects, and authentic service learning.

4. Teachers and students connect local issues with the broad concepts of social studies. Teachers encourage students to explore specific social issues that impact their lives, to ask questions, and to pursue their own answers within the context of broader social studies questions and topics.

5. Teachers, students, and staff participate in community events that encourage students to make informed and reasoned decisions for the public good as citizens of a culturally diverse, democratic society.

6. Teachers display student work that provides evidence of social science research and learning in public areas of the school.

D. Assessing Social Studies

1. Teachers create opportunities for students to demonstrate understanding of concepts by explaining them accurately to others using graphic representations, models, or demonstrations.

2. Teachers regularly check for understanding and misconceptions. They support students in tracking their own progress toward learning targets and provide feedback that gets students back "on track" toward targets.

3. Teachers debrief learning by inviting students to generalize and apply concepts and procedures to other contexts and problems. They encourage students to reflect on what they learned, how they learned it, and how they can transfer it to new contexts.

4. Teachers use multiple methods of assessment, including one-on-one discussions, interactive notebooks, performances, or products that result from projects, as well as quizzes and tests.

Core Practice 18
Teaching in and through the Arts

In the EL Education model, arts are celebrated as a central aspect of learning and life. Schools teach art as an academic discipline and also in core academic subjects, where it engages students in problem solving, planning, and perseverance. They celebrate the unique capacity of the arts to express truth, beauty, and joy. Student exhibitions of learning feature the arts along with other subjects. Schools are filled with student artwork, which is displayed in a way that honors the work. Artistic performances are points of pride for the school. Arts are often used as a window into disciplinary content in other academic subjects (e.g., ancient Greek architecture as an entry point to ancient Greek civilization, protest songs as a case study when learning about the civil rights movement). The arts also provide opportunities to explore diverse cultures, perspectives, and regions of the world.

The visual and performing arts are taught using the same effective instructional practices that are used in other disciplines, and all students have access to professional artists and professional exhibitions and performances. Ideally, specialists in visual and performance arts are on the school staff. If they are not, classroom teachers use professional art educators and artists whenever possible to support high-caliber artistic learning. Teachers and students analyze professional and student-created work models as the basis for understanding what excellence looks like and sounds like in the particular form. Through critique and revision, students render works of art that demonstrate complexity, craftsmanship, and authenticity.

The arts build school culture and student character by emphasizing risk-taking, creativity, and a quest for beauty and meaning. Teachers invite students to make artistic choices and design opportunities for students to make independent decisions that are purposeful and meaningful. Students work through diverse arts traditions to reshape the arts, the world, and themselves.

A. Planning for Arts Instruction

1. School leaders and teachers identify many opportunities for art instruction, including visual and performing arts classes, as well as art projects conducted in other disciplines. These are aligned with art and disciplinary standards and documented in schoolwide and course curriculum maps.

2. Teachers craft standards-aligned learning targets that address knowledge, skills, and character traits related to the study of art.

3. When selecting case studies or designing projects or learning expeditions in non-art classes, teachers often include art as a focus of study or a product of the learning. When designing curriculum, teachers consider the following questions:

   a. What is the scope and focus of the project? Examples of scope and focus include:

      i. The arts or history of the arts as the primary focus of a learning expedition (e.g., arts in the Harlem Renaissance, in which each case study examines a different artistic genre—jazz, painting, poetry)

      ii. The arts or history of the arts as the subject of a case study within a larger project or learning expedition (e.g., the Ashcan School of painting during a study of the early 20th century)

   b. Does the project and product require students to both learn the techniques of an artistic medium and to represent their understanding through art?

   c. What is the authentic audience for the artistic product? These may include galleries, public performance venues, events, or publications.

4. Teachers select and evaluate texts to support instruction in the arts. These may include photographs, videos (e.g., of dance), or a three-dimensional artwork that can serve as a "text" that students "read" and interpret.

5. Teachers plan lessons with the product or problem in mind and design a process that supports students to create the product or solve the problem. They choose lesson structures and protocols (e.g., Workshop 2.0, critique protocols) that give students opportunities to practice the skills they need to create the artwork or that enable students to analyze the problem, experiment with artistic materials and methods, and create solutions (e.g., discovery-based lessons).

6. Teachers, particularly when not artists themselves, identify experts and fieldwork opportunities that can augment in-class art instruction.

7. Teachers in non-art disciplines and art teachers collaborate to design assessments that address disciplinary concepts, artistic standards, and character targets related to creativity, collaboration, and perseverance.

B. Teaching Artistic Techniques

1. Teachers sequence lessons to support students in building knowledge about the history of the art form as well as skills and techniques required for a particular product. They provide ample time for all students to practice, revise, and polish artistic work.

2. Teachers convey the symbol system and domain-specific vocabulary used in the particular art form they are teaching (e.g., notation in music).

3. Teachers include lessons that focus on character learning targets with special relevance in the arts (e.g., precision, perseverance, practice, or imaginative play).

4. Teachers conduct critique lessons based on student-created or professional models that include:

   a. Developing criteria for excellence in conversation with students that reflect disciplinary standards and unpacking the attributes of quality work: complexity, craftsmanship, and authenticity

   b. Creating rubrics that communicate those criteria to students as the basis for evaluation

5. Teachers provide many opportunities for students to reflect on and self-assess the quality of their work based on feedback. (See also *Core Practice 12: Planning and Supporting High-Quality Student Work.*)

   a. Teachers instruct students how to give and receive feedback on their own and each other's work based on clear expectations and criteria.

   b. Teachers provide feedback on works in progress and on the skills students are practicing in class.

   c. When appropriate, students revise multiple times based on feedback.

6. Teachers design opportunities for student choice and expression. They challenge students to work in established artistic forms and also to put artistic forms to new uses or work with multimodal or interdisciplinary forms.

7. Teachers differentiate supports and offer students flexibility in their approach based on differences in students' needs and interests. Individual students have clear roles and responsibilities for collaborative art products so that they can be assessed individually as well as collectively.

8. Teachers teach the presentation and performance skills needed for displaying or presenting the work to an authentic audience. Student art is often accompanied by artists' statements or reflections so that artistic thinking can be demonstrated to the public and is a part of learning and assessment (e.g., on gallery walls and in programs for musical, movement, or drama performances).

C. Creating a Culture of Art

1. Teachers provide opportunities for all students to learn about and experience the arts through live performances, galleries, and exhibitions and to work in a variety of media.

2. The school celebrates the beauty and power of art in all forms. Arts instruction builds and celebrates students' understanding of culture—students' own culture and others' culture—through art.

   a. The school building is rich with original student artwork, which is curated and displayed in a way that honors the work.

   b. Whenever artistic products or performances are included in learning expeditions or projects, the artistic work is treated with integrity and valued equally with non-artistic products.

   c. Teachers, leaders, students, and families take pride in performances.

   d. Documentation panels of student learning, displayed throughout the school, are strong works of art in themselves.

D. Assessing Art Products

1. Teachers and students value artistic work as academic achievement. Students include artistic work and reflections in portfolios for student-led conferences and passage presentations.

2. Teachers assess final products based on artistic criteria or disciplinary standards and on character learning targets relevant to artistic endeavors, such as creativity, craftsmanship, or perseverance.

Core Practice 19

Differentiating Instruction

In the EL Education model, differentiation is a philosophical belief and an instructional approach through which teachers proactively plan instruction to capitalize on students' varied assets and meet students' varied needs based upon ongoing assessment. Teachers differentiate for students with disabilities, for advanced learners, for English language learners (see also *Core Practice 20: Teaching English Language Learners*), and for students whose differences are not formally evaluated but have been identified through informal learning and interest inventories. In whole group general education instruction, teachers use flexible groupings of students and design respectful tasks that allow for different approaches to the same goals. Teachers build a culture that honors diverse assets and needs and holds all students accountable to the same long-term learning targets, putting equity at the center of the school's commitment and vision. At the same time, general education teachers make accommodations and modifications for students who have identified exceptionalities and collaborate with a team of school professionals to provide additional supports or extensions.

A. Schoolwide Structures to Support Differentiated Instruction

1. School leaders ensure that students with disabilities and advanced learners (together these two groups compose *exceptional learners*) are taught in general education classrooms to the greatest extent possible.

2. School leaders ensure that a continuum of services for exceptional learners is available based on the needs of the student population that is served. These services, to the greatest extent possible, are provided via a push-in delivery model.

3. School leaders ensure that supplemental services that provide for additional support, intervention, or extension are available to students whose needs are not being met via the general education classroom or within the continuum of services for exceptional learners.

4. A multidisciplinary team (e.g., exceptional children's specialists, school counselors, classroom teachers) guides decision-making to serve the needs of exceptional learners and maximize their contributions. These decisions include:

   a. Making sensitive decisions about placement and services that are informed by psychological evaluations and other high-quality assessments, including assessment of students' mastery of knowledge and skills, character, and work samples

   b. Considering the needs of students who fall into multiple need categories (e.g., English language learners who are also advanced learners) and identifying services that meet all needs

   c. Ensuring that all staff are equipped to fully include exceptional children in the school community

   d. Using research-based best practices to support exceptional learners

   e. Providing adequate planning time to collaborative teams who support this student population

   f. Providing all staff with high-quality professional learning related to meeting the needs of exceptional learners

   g. Developing and training effective teams (e.g., Multi-Tier System of Supports) to ensure that students needing supplemental support are identified and that placement in interventions and other programs are made appropriately

5. A multidisciplinary team develops accommodations and modifications with student and family input as a function of the student's Individualized Education Program (IEP). The intention of accommodations and modifications is to achieve the most rigorous outcome in the least restrictive environment possible for the student.

6. Leaders, school counselors, teachers, and exceptional learning specialists consider college and career an option for all students and prepare students with disabilities to seek the best postsecondary option. They teach self-advocacy skills and help students understand their learning challenges, assets, and strengths.

B. Differentiating Instruction

1. School leaders and teachers ensure that to the greatest extent possible, exceptional learners complete the same curriculum and meet the same learning targets as their classmates in the general education classroom with same-age peers.

2. Teachers of exceptional learners and general education teachers collaborate to plan and deliver differentiated instruction for exceptional learners that meet IEP goals. They determine student needs and readiness through use of multiple assessment strategies (e.g.,

Differentiating Instruction (continued)

pre-assessments, student self-assessments, inventories, providing multiple opportunities for success).

3. Teachers in general education classrooms employ flexible grouping that is:

   a. Informed by multiple and ongoing assessment instead of stagnant ability grouping (i.e., tracking)

   b. Grouped heterogeneously or homogeneously depending on the purpose of the lesson and the task students are given (e.g., a task that calls for collaboration between diverse perspectives likely calls for heterogeneous groups; a mathematics lesson in which some students need additional or different guided instruction and others need a more complex challenge may require homogeneous groupings)

4. Teachers select materials so that all students read high-quality literature and complex informational text appropriate for grade-level standards (unless an IEP dictates otherwise).

   a. For students with reading disabilities or specific learning disabilities that impact reading, differentiated texts are used strategically rather than as a permanent substitute for grade-level texts.

   b. All students also have access to texts that respond to their interests and academic readiness.

5. Teachers strategically work with small groups to build content knowledge, context, or skills in advance of whole group instruction when this strategy enhances students' ability to enter the whole group lesson.

6. Teachers provide multiple pathways for meeting the learning targets based on student readiness (e.g., allowing more time for students with disabilities to practice or providing a more complex grapple problem for advanced learners).

7. Teachers provide supplemental or differentiated materials so that students with disabilities can fully participate in the learning (e.g., visual cues, graphic organizers, smaller chunks of complex text, vocabulary guides).

8. Teachers provide opportunities for all students to participate in all aspects of the curriculum and interact with their peers to develop compassion and empathy.

9. Teachers are intentional about selecting diverse texts that build in and build on student interests, backgrounds, and choices. They are sensitive to cultural differences and backgrounds.

10. Teachers design lessons to ensure that all students have access to the background knowledge, vocabulary, grammar, and academic language needed to succeed.

C. Creating a Culture for Differentiated Instruction

1. Leaders and teachers verbalize and model a commitment to equity and diversity within the school by doing the following:

   a. Celebrating diversity and practicing inclusion in school events and traditions (e.g., providing accommodations so that students with disabilities can participate in fieldwork)

   b. Ensuring that all students have access and are exposed to cultural and social opportunities (e.g., libraries, museums, universities)

   c. Honoring the best work of all students, not just students whose work is exemplary

   d. Teaching lessons that help students understand the diversity of students at their school

   e. Learning about the home, cultural, and community backgrounds of their students

   f. Sharing their own home, cultural, and community background with students when this is in the service of creating an inclusive classroom community

2. Teachers track patterns of student participation in classroom discussions and teacher/student interaction. They use these data to adjust instruction to ensure equitable participation and interaction.

3. Leaders track patterns of family participation in decision-making about exceptional learners. They use these data to adjust school procedures, structures, and policies to ensure equitable participation and interaction.

Core Practice 20
Teaching English Language Learners

The EL Education model recognizes that all speakers of English, at whatever level of proficiency, are constantly learning English. Some learners of English are acquiring it as a second, third, or fourth language, and rather than viewing bi- or multilingualism as a problem to be solved, leaders and teachers create a school and classroom culture to optimize it as an asset.

Teachers of English language learners (ELLs) assess students' understanding of English and school background in order to differentiate appropriately for the diversity of ELLs. In all subject areas, they use instructional approaches (e.g., Language Dives, Conversation Cues) that immerse ELLs in rich classroom discourse and support language acquisition as well as knowledge and skills development. They strive to assess ELLs' knowledge and skills separately from their language skills. They value language diversity and honor students' home languages and cultures by creating opportunities for ELLs and language-minority students to teach their peers and take pride in their languages and cultures.

A. Schoolwide Structures to Support English Language Learners

1. While ELLs are learning English, they have a wide variety of school backgrounds, reading abilities (in their home language and in English), and social and emotional skills based on diverse experiences. Therefore, leaders and teachers establish policies to ensure that ELLs are taught in regular education, heterogeneous classrooms to the greatest extent possible.

2. Leaders ensure that the school offers a continuum of services (both co-taught and small group instruction) to strategically support ELLs. When needed, leaders also ensure supplemental services, such as translators and newcomer support.

3. Leaders and teachers communicate with families and students in ways that reflect students' linguistic needs.

4. Leaders' and teachers' decisions about placement and programs for ELLs are based on researched high-quality assessments and consultation with families. A multidisciplinary team considers the needs of students who fall into multiple need categories (e.g., ELLs who are also advanced learners).

5. School leaders and ELL teachers ensure that all staff members are equipped to fully include multilingual students in the school community, both meeting these students' needs and maximizing their contributions.

    a. School leaders, general education teachers, and ELL teachers use research-based best practices to support second-language acquisition.

    b. Collaborative teams that work with ELLs are provided with adequate planning time to support this student population.

    c. School leaders and learning specialists provide all staff with high-quality professional learning related to meeting the needs of English language learners.

6. Leaders and teachers advocate for district and other standardized assessments to be fair and unbiased toward ELLs.

B. Teaching English Language Learners

1. In general education classes, ELLs work toward the same learning targets as their peers.

    a. Students work on the same final product, but teachers differentiate supports for getting to the product (e.g., as ELLs compose a letter to the editor, they may use sentence frames to shape the expression of their thoughts).

    b. ELL teachers collaborate with general education teachers to plan and deliver differentiated instruction for English language learners based on the range of language proficiency levels. They write additional learning targets for ELLs that address language development (e.g., "I can contrast my position with another using comparative adjectives").

    c. Teachers determine student needs and readiness through use of multiple assessment strategies (e.g., pre-assessments, student self-assessments, inventories, providing multiple opportunities for success). They recognize that ELLs may be strong in one subject area and not in another.

2. General education teachers include ELLs in heterogeneous groupings or flexible groupings based on their readiness for the skill or content being taught. Sometimes it may be appropriate to group ELLs together for differentiated instruction, such as for an additional Language Dive.

3. Teachers use compelling and challenging instructional materials. They provide supplemental materials so that ELLs can access content (e.g., conversations about the language and meaning of complex text, visual cues, materials written in the student's home language, vocabulary guides, culturally relevant materials).

4. Teachers use protocols and Conversation Cues to engage ELLs in the complex oral conversation of classroom discourse. Conversation Cues encourage students to:

   a. Talk and be understood (e.g., "Can you say more about that?")

   b. Listen carefully to one another and seek to understand (e.g., "Who can repeat what your classmate said?")

   c. Deepen their thinking (e.g., "Why do you think that?")

   d. Think with others to expand conversation (e.g., "Who can add on to what your classmate said?")

5. Teachers guide students to notice and think about how language is used by conducting Language Dives, brief structured conversations in which students analyze and practice complex sentences, grammatical structures, collocations, and idiomatic expressions in context. Language Dives may involve the whole class or only ELLs.

6. Teachers track global, pervasive, or stigmatizing errors and give students measured feedback that addresses errors. Equally, they praise students' efforts as a sign of beneficial risk-taking and growth.

7. Teachers give students ample writing practice so that they become familiar with writing expectations and have multiple opportunities to construct sentences and paragraphs in English as well as in conversation.

8. Teachers help students learn and practice vocabulary within the context of the topic they are teaching and the text they are using. They discuss and practice using common academic phrases.

9. When designing assessments of content knowledge or skill, teachers work to separate mastery from the ability to express that mastery in English.

C. Creating a Culture for English Language Learning

1. Leaders and teachers honor students' home languages and cultures through the school's environment, communications, and organizational structures.

   a. Members of the school community celebrate diversity and practice inclusion in school events and traditions. They celebrate not only ethnically different holidays, but also the values, beliefs, approaches, and interactions of multicultural students.

   b. Leaders and teachers ensure that school signage and other critical communications to students and families are accessible to ELLs and their families.

   c. Leaders make sure that the front office staff is trained and equipped to connect and reach out to multicultural families. This includes practices such as calling home in the preferred language and identifying people at the school who speak various languages and can be available to translate at meetings and conferences.

2. Leaders provide multiple ways for families of ELLs to engage with the school, including serving on decision-making committees, actively participating in classrooms as experts, and assisting with schoolwide events.

3. Teachers learn about the home, cultural, and community backgrounds of their students. They may share their own home, cultural, and community background with students in the service of creating an inclusive classroom community.

4. Teachers honor students' home language learning in tandem with English. They encourage families to help their children develop literacy and other complex academic uses of their home language.

5. Teachers learn words and phrases in their students' home languages and publicly honor multilingualism by posting words and phrases in anchor charts or other visuals in the classroom.

6. Crew leaders teach lessons that focus on understanding the diversity of languages that are spoken in their school, just as they support understanding of other forms of diversity.

Culture and Character

The EL Education model fosters and celebrates students' character development by building a culture in which students and staff work together to become effective learners and ethical people who contribute to a better world. Schools establish Habits of Character—qualities like respect, responsibility, courage, and kindness—and model and discuss them every day. The school is suffused by a spirit of Crew: students and staff work together as a team to sustain a learning community where everyone belongs and can succeed.

Core Practices in This Domain

- Creating a Community of Learning
- Fostering Habits of Character
- Building the Culture and Structure of Crew
- Engaging Families and the Community in the Life of the School
- Creating Beautiful Spaces That Promote Learning
- Promoting Courage and Adventure

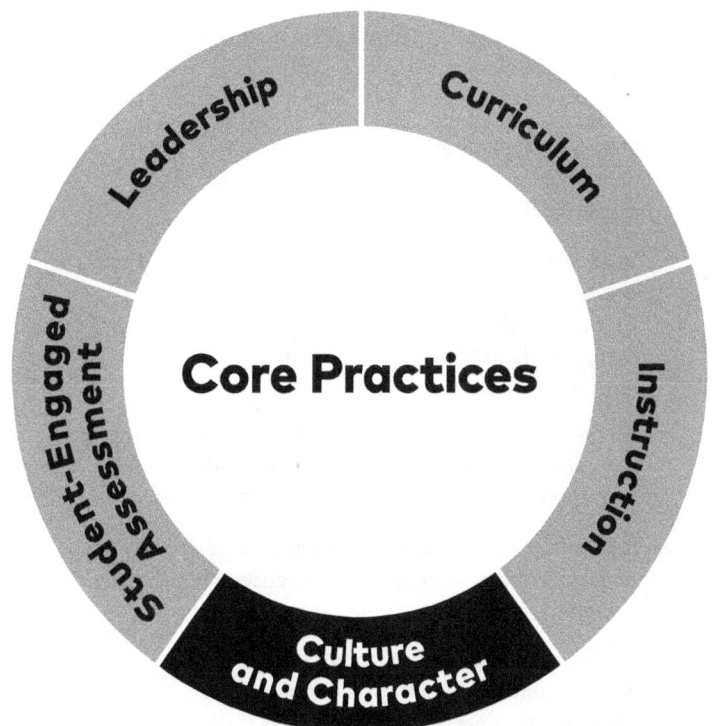

Core Practice 21
Creating a Community of Learning

The EL Education model fosters and celebrates students' academic growth and character development as inseparable. Members of the school community live up to the spirit of EL Education's Design Principles on a daily basis and create a school climate characterized by physical and emotional safety, joy in learning, kindness, and positive leadership. All adults in the school communicate clear expectations for student character based on the school's Habits of Character and model those values in their own practice and interactions. Policies and practices encourage students to become effective learners and ethical people who contribute to a better world. This means leaders, teachers, and students value diversity and work to create a community that is equitable, inclusive, and committed to social justice.

A. Setting Clear Schoolwide Expectations

1. School leaders, teachers, and students adopt Habits of Character to which all students and staff members aspire. When choosing and naming the Habits of Character (e.g., respect, responsibility, perseverance, courage, compassion), leaders and teachers:

   a. Prioritize social and emotional learning equally with academic learning

   b. Choose habits that support students to become effective learners, ethical people, and contributors to a better world

2. The school adopts a subset of Habits of Character connected to becoming effective learners, called Habits of Scholarship or Habits of Work (e.g., I come to class prepared; I participate actively in class; I complete my homework; I collaborate with classmates). These habits are assessed and reported separately from academic learning targets. (See also *Core Practice 22: Fostering Habits of Character*.)

3. Leaders and teachers establish practices that develop student accountability for and celebrate Habits of Character, including the following actions:

   a. Leaders and teachers make Habits of Character visible across the school. They frequently discuss Habits of Character with staff and students and incorporate them into the fabric of school life, such as daily Crew meetings.

   b. All members of the school community hold themselves and each other accountable for upholding the Habits of Character.

   c. Students reflect on Habits of Character and share their progress in student led-conferences and passage portfolios.

   d. Leaders and teachers recognize character in school awards, community circles, and other public acknowledgments.

   e. Leaders and teachers use the Habits of Character as the foundation of a positive approach to discipline and restorative justice.

4. Teachers partner with students to translate Habits of Character into specific behaviors called norms (e.g., leave no trace, embrace challenge as an opportunity, speak and act with compassion). Norms may be specific to a classroom, setting, or event and also may include general schoolwide norms. Teachers ensure that students agree upon norms in which Habits of Character can flourish.

5. Leaders and teachers explicitly model, teach, and refer to the Habits of Character in classrooms and throughout the school (in the lunchroom, halls, recess, before and after school).

   a. Leaders and teachers use the school's common language for Habits of Character.

   b. Teachers support students to make connections between Habits of Character and their academic and life success.

   c. Teachers and leaders frequently refer to norms and Habits of Character when praising or redirecting students' behavior.

   d. Leaders and teachers model the Habits of Character with students and in their professional relationships.

B. Fostering a Positive Climate for Learning

1. Leaders and teachers model and reinforce the following academic mindsets:

   a. I belong in this academic community.

   b. My ability and competence grow with my effort.

   c. I can succeed at this.

   d. This work has value for me.

2. Teachers and leaders act as models of lifelong learning for students.

a. When appropriate, teachers discuss their own learning with students.

b. Leaders create dedicated time for teachers' professional learning. They communicate it to families and celebrate it in the school community.

3. Leaders and teachers ensure that all school members are implicitly and explicitly included and supported in the learning community. They show respect and use inclusive behaviors toward students and staff regardless of background or identity.

4. Leaders and teachers manage their nonverbal communication, voice, and emotions in ways that communicate to students that it is OK to seek support for challenges.

5. Leaders and teachers foster student self-management and responsibility for learning through the following actions:

a. Looking for opportunities to elevate student voice and leadership in the classroom and across the school

b. Framing redirection in terms of restoration of the learning community (e.g., "When you follow our classroom norm of respecting diverse perspectives, you can rejoin the discussion circle.")

c. Establishing classroom norms that describe what responsibility for learning, collaborative and compassionate behavior, and positive leadership look like and sound like in the specific context of the classroom

d. Establishing routines and procedures (e.g., jobs, transition procedures, nonverbal signals, materials organizational systems) that foster student independence and competence

e. Using established structures, programs, or practices (e.g., restorative circles, peer support) to engage students in determining logical and consistent consequences for student actions that disrupt the learning environment

6. Leaders and teachers treat challenging behaviors as a learning opportunity for both students and teachers.

a. Leaders and teachers examine discipline policies and practices for hidden biases and work to implement discipline equitably.

b. Leaders and teachers actively seek to understand causes of challenging behaviors and conflict.

c. Leaders and teachers understand and discuss with staff and students the concept of growth mindset—the idea that ability is not fixed and that through challenging work and strategic practice, individuals can grow.

d. Leaders and teachers develop affirming, positive behavior intervention systems to minimize suspensions. They avoid zero tolerance policies that exclude students from the learning environment.

e. Leaders and teachers address lapses in good character explicitly, respectfully, and well, even if it means, for example, interrupting class work or a staff meeting.

f. Leaders and teachers identify consequences for challenging behaviors that give students opportunities to own their mistakes, repair harm to individuals and the learning environment, and rejoin the learning community (e.g., restorative circles, peer support or judiciary councils, restitution through service).

g. Leaders and teachers clearly document and communicate consequences to students, families, and other staff.

C. Building Traditions

1. Leaders and teachers create traditions that celebrate Habits of Character in whole-school settings and in classrooms (e.g., public acknowledgements in community circles, inspirational readings in Crew).

2. Leaders and teachers customize EL Education traditions. They develop the school's own unique traditions that express the school's vision of a positive community that is focused on learning.

3. Students play an active role in maintaining school traditions and acting as leaders (e.g., being ambassadors for visitors, leading meetings, maintaining the building, mentoring younger children, leading morning announcements).

4. Leaders and teachers consider how school spaces and rituals accommodate various traditions and reflect a culture of community, respect, and joy in learning. They ensure that spaces used for school traditions and celebrations are safe and inclusive and communicate the school's values.

Fostering Habits of Character

In the EL Education model, students' character development is equally as important as producing high-quality work and mastering knowledge and skills. Throughout their educational journey, students are working to become effective learners, ethical people, and contributors to a better world. Schools adopt Habits of Scholarship, which are a subset of Habits of Character that support students to become effective learners. They articulate Habits of Character that enable students to become ethical people, which include traits like respect, honesty, and compassion. They articulate Habits of Character that enable students to contribute to a better world through service and stewardship.

All three aspects of strong character (becoming effective learners, becoming ethical people, and contributing to a better world) are essential for success in school and in life. In the EL Education model, all learning is character-based. Students are on a mission to do good work: work that is good in quality, good for the soul, and good for the world.

A. Becoming Effective Learners (through Habits of Scholarship)

1. Leaders and teachers adopt a subset of Habits of Character connected to becoming effective learners, called Habits of Scholarship or Habits of Work.

   a. Teachers post Habits of Scholarship in classrooms.

   b. Teachers discuss Habits of Scholarship regularly.

2. Leaders and teachers articulate, in student-friendly language, what Habits of Scholarship look like and sound like. They design rubrics, anchor charts, and other supporting documents that can be easily referenced by teachers, students, and the greater community.

3. Leaders and teachers reference the school's Habits of Scholarship in school structures and documents (e.g., portfolios, school handbooks, transcripts, celebrations of learning).

4. Teachers explicitly plan lessons, experiences, and assessment opportunities (both qualitative and quantitative) that support students in developing their Habits of Scholarship.

   a. Teachers provide many opportunities for students to practice Habits of Scholarship in daily lessons, projects, fieldwork, and Crew.

   b. Teachers intentionally teach behaviors that enable students to develop Habits of Scholarship (e.g., note taking, recording homework, revising, accessing resources independently).

   c. Teachers unpack Habits of Scholarship into a purposeful progression of developmentally appropriate character learning targets (e.g., "I can revise my work to achieve high-quality products"). Students and teachers track students' growth and mastery of these targets.

   d. Teachers name and honor students' Habits of Scholarship to reinforce these behaviors in specific settings.

   e. Teachers create instructional routines and opportunities for reflection on Habits of Scholarship.

5. Students regularly track their progress on Habits of Scholarship and can articulate the link between their Habits of Scholarship and future success in school, career, and life.

6. Teachers assess Habits of Scholarship separately from academic targets.

7. Leaders and teachers publicly celebrate students who exhibit strong or improving Habits of Scholarship.

B. Becoming Ethical People

1. Leaders and teachers include in the school's Habits of Character traits that support students in becoming ethical people (e.g., kindness, honesty, empathy, respect).

2. Leaders and teachers work with students to articulate, in student-friendly language, what working to become an ethical person looks like and sounds like. These descriptions are often embedded in schoolwide and classroom norms.

3. Leaders and teachers model Habits of Character across classrooms and content areas and in professional conversations. A focus on ethical behavior is seen not as time away from learning, but as highly valuable and an investment in student achievement.

4. Leaders and teachers explicitly plan experiences that address Habits of Scholarship for Crew, classrooms, and the school as a whole. They support students in becoming ethical people through the following actions:

a. Providing many opportunities for students to practice empathy, honesty, respect, and compassion in daily lessons, projects, fieldwork, and Crew

b. Supporting students' agency and self-efficacy by encouraging students to become allies and "upstanders" who reject and confront behaviors that disrupt a respectful culture (e.g., bullying, discrimination, name-calling, cliques)

c. Explicitly teaching team-building, conflict resolution, problem solving, and personal communication skills

d. Crafting and using character targets for academic lessons (e.g., "I can listen actively to diverse opinions")

e. Naming and honoring students' ethical behavior to reinforce what it looks like and sounds like in specific settings

5. Students regularly self-assess how they are working to become ethical people. Students document their Habits of Character qualitatively with examples and other evidence in reflections. They can articulate the link between their Habits of Character and their relationships in the community.

6. Leaders and teachers create traditions that honor the culture of respect, honesty, and inclusion. They celebrate teachers and students who treat others with fairness and compassion and stand up for what is right.

C. Contributing to a Better World

1. Leaders and teachers include in the school's Habits of Character traits that support students in contributing to a better world and becoming global citizens. These include valuing diversity and working toward greater equity, inclusion, and social justice.

2. Leaders and teachers work with students to articulate, in student-friendly language, what contributing to a better world looks like and sounds like. These descriptions of civic character are often embedded in schoolwide and classroom norms.

3. Leaders and teachers model civic character through acts of service within and beyond the school.

4. Leaders and teachers collaborate with students to analyze and evaluate school and community structures and traditions and to revise them to create a more diverse, equitable, and inclusive community.

5. Leaders and teachers design curricula that teach civic character and provide students with opportunities to contribute to building a better world.

a. Teachers focus on local and global issues that invite students to solve real-world problems in case studies, projects, and learning expeditions. Student-created products often contribute something of value for readers, viewers, or listeners (e.g., a student-written oral history of local war veterans). Projects frequently include a service component.

b. Crew leaders support students to plan and conduct service projects. They provide students with opportunities to make decisions, become leaders, contribute to local and global communities, and build more equitable communities.

c. Schools offer extracurricular opportunities for students to lead or contribute to service-oriented initiatives.

6. Students document their work and service from classwork, Crew, or extracurricular activities.

7. Leaders and teachers publicly celebrate service, civic engagement, and global citizenship in school traditions, events, and communications.

Core Practice 23
Building the Culture and Structure of Crew

In the EL Education model, the tradition of Crew is both a *culture* and a *structure*. The term "crew" comes from educator Kurt Hahn, founder of Outward Bound. Hahn's quote "We are crew, not passengers, strengthened by acts of consequential service to others" inspired the EL Education motto, "We are crew." The culture of crew impels all members of a school community to work together as a team, to pitch in, to help others. Staff and students help their colleagues and peers get up the mountain together—individual success is not enough. The structure of Crew—daily meetings to support everyone's learning and growth—makes time for students to build meaningful relationships with peers and their Crew leader, to reflect on and monitor academic progress, and to focus on character development. Crew is also an engine for equity and inclusion, a place where all students feel they belong and can succeed. Crew leaders strategically plan Crew meetings to address and assess these multiple goals.

Other school structures can also help build crew culture and ensure that every student is well known and supported by peers and adults (e.g., community meetings, mentoring, peer counseling, restorative justice work, apprenticeships). The culture of crew extends beyond the school walls to relationships with families and community members.

A. Fostering a Culture of Crew among Staff

1. Leaders and teachers establish a culture of crew among staff that supports and is a model for the culture of crew among students.

2. Leaders and teachers ensure that every staff member feels respected and valued as part of the culture of crew, as well as supported to grow personally and professionally. (See also *Core Practice 34: Cultivating a Positive Professional Culture*.)

3. Leaders and teachers create structures and strategies to cultivate a positive culture among staff (e.g., orientation, mentoring, communication norms, team-building activities, readings, staff events that build relationships, appreciation traditions).

4. Leaders and teachers create systems to overcome challenges to a positive culture of crew (e.g., conversation protocols for discussion of diversity and equity, including staff members' own backgrounds and identities; equitable decision-making processes; protocols for conflict resolution among staff or in response to school crises).

5. Leaders and teachers plan staff Crew meetings to fit the school community (e.g., whole staff Crew meetings, grade/ team or department Crew meetings, mixed small groups from across the building that meet regularly as staff Crews).

6. Staff Crew meetings (or the crew components of staff meetings) are focused not on the "business" of school, but on staff relationships, emotional health, growth, and sustainability.

7. Leaders and teachers sometimes use staff Crew as a structure to prepare staff to lead a student Crew effectively.

Professional learning for Crew facilitation includes:

a. Providing a Crew curriculum framework

b. Providing sample Crew lessons or a Crew lesson format

c. Teaching greetings and debrief strategies

d. Modeling effective Crew facilitation (e.g., circling up, greetings, initiatives)

e. Teaching specific team-building activities

f. Teaching strategies for relationship-building, conflict resolution, and courageous conversations

g. Addressing questions and concerns about Crew

B. Fostering a Culture of Crew among Students

1. Leaders and teachers ensure that every student has a Crew leader who gets to know that student well and serves as an advocate for the student's academic and social progress.

2. Leaders and teachers use a variety of structures and strategies to get to know students well (e.g., Crew time, home visits, flexible grouping, regular check-ins). They foster a culture of crew by supporting students to make friends, be heard, and interact as contributing members of the school community.

a. Leaders and teachers create structures for welcoming new students who arrive midyear.

b. Leaders and teachers foster multiyear connections between students of different ages and between students and adults in school and in the community. These connections may take the form of reading buddies, tutoring, mentoring, internships, apprenticeships, or other partnerships.

c. Leaders and teachers support students to feel safe, valued, respected, and included regardless of background or identity.

d. Leaders and teachers support all students to succeed and hold them accountable for high academic expectations.

3. Leaders and teachers celebrate the contributions of members of the learning community through community meetings, events, and other traditions.

C. Crew as a Structure in Primary and Elementary Classrooms

1. In primary and elementary classrooms, teachers generally serve as Crew leaders for their entire class. They typically hold Crew meetings daily at the beginning of the day (sometimes referred to as "morning meeting") and sometimes also at the end of the day.

2. Whenever possible, students in Crew sit or stand in a circle so they can see and hear each other without the interference of furniture. A circle allows Crew members to be equally vulnerable, connected, and supportive of one another.

3. Teachers as Crew leaders plan and facilitate Crew experiences that support building relationships, Habits of Character, literacy, portfolio work, adventure, and service learning.

    a. Crew leaders incorporate greetings, stories, appreciations, apologies, and other activities that foster students' sense of purpose, belonging, and agency.

    b. Crew leaders engage students in collaboration and competition in a joyful, supportive environment (e.g., through the use of team-building initiatives and cooperative problem-solving games). They debrief initiatives by helping students reflect on skills and mindsets that can be applied beyond the activity.

    c. Crew leaders facilitate student reflection on their Habits of Character. Positive behavior is celebrated. Concerns about behavior (e.g., discourtesy, bullying, exclusion, or not following classroom norms) are often addressed in Crew, sometimes through restorative circles or other conflict mediation strategies.

    d. Crew leaders facilitate student reflection on the relationship among their academic progress, Habits of Scholarship, and quality of their work. Often, students work on portfolios or prepare for student-led conferences in Crew.

    e. Crew leaders help students understand foundational concepts of EL Education, such as the concept of "crew, not passengers," the Design Principles, growth mindset, and Habits of Character.

4. Crew leaders form positive relationships with parents and other care providers, monitor academic progress, and lead interventions as needed so that every student knows that he/she can be a successful member of the Crew.

D. Crew as a Structure in Secondary Classrooms

1. Leaders and teachers establish a schedule that allows for Crew to meet on a consistent basis for a significant amount of time (30 to 60 minutes) most days of the week, every day if possible. (Crew is structured similarly to what some schools call "advisory.")

2. Leaders and teachers develop a schoolwide Crew curriculum with the following features:

    a. Includes learning targets, common lessons, common procedures, and tools for progress monitoring

    b. Designates specific purposes for Crew on different days or for different grade levels (e.g., literacy on Tuesdays, college preparation for juniors)

    c. Provides consistency in Crews across the school but also allows for individual Crew leaders to craft or customize lessons for Crew members

    d. Provides a pathway for college preparation (e.g., college visits, college research, applications, financial forms, interview preparation)

3. Leaders and teachers are careful to keep Crews small (8 to 15 students), so that students can fully participate and develop meaningful relationships with their peers and Crew leaders. Often staff beyond classroom teachers are trained and supported to be Crew leaders (e.g., athletic coaches, office staff, custodians, counselors).

4. Leaders and teachers determine how students are grouped for Crew in the way the school feels works best. Often Crews stay together over multiple years and Crew leaders stay with one Crew for multiple years (e.g., three years of middle school; four years of high school).

5. Crew is not homeroom. Crew leaders plan and prepare for meaningful lessons with learning targets. Students are active participants and leaders in Crew. In many schools, Crew is a credit-bearing, graded course. High school juniors and seniors use Crew to prepare for college admissions and postsecondary life.

6. Teachers as Crew leaders plan and facilitate Crew experiences that address healthy relationships, Habits of Character, literacy, portfolio work, adventure, and service learning.

    a. Crew leaders incorporate greetings, stories, appreciations, apologies, and other activities that foster students' sense of purpose, belonging, and agency.

b. Crew leaders engage students in collaboration and competition in a joyful, supportive environment (e.g., through the use of team-building initiatives and cooperative problem-solving games). They debrief initiatives by helping students reflect on skills and mindsets that can be applied beyond the activity.

c. Crew leaders facilitate student reflection on their Habits of Character. Positive behavior is celebrated. Concerns about behavior (e.g., discourtesy, bullying, exclusion, or not following classroom norms) are often addressed in Crew, sometimes through restorative circles or other conflict mediation strategies.

d. Crew leaders facilitate student reflection on the relationship among their academic progress, Habits of Scholarship, and quality of their work. Students often work on portfolios or prepare for student-led conferences in Crew.

e. Crew leaders help students understand foundational concepts of EL Education, such as the concept of "crew, not passengers," the Design Principles, growth mindset, and Habits of Character.

7. Crew leaders ensure that all their students know about and have access to demanding academic courses, extracurricular activities, academic and social supports, and the best sequence of classes for college placement or postgraduation pursuits.

8. Crew leaders guide and support the college application process for students, including financial aid and scholarships, especially for first-generation college applicants. School counselors support Crew leaders in this work.

9. Crew leaders form positive relationships with parents and other care providers, monitor academic progress, and facilitate conversations between students, care providers, and other staff members as needed so that every student knows that he/she can be a successful member of the Crew and is ready for graduation.

Core Practice 24

Engaging Families and the Community in the Life of the School

Families are key partners in the education of their children. In the EL Education model, staff members make families welcome, value their contributions and backgrounds, and engage them actively in the life of the school. Leaders and teachers explicitly recognize that families care about their children's education, bring strengths, and add value to the community. Leaders and teachers communicate with families regularly and respectfully and provide multiple ways to contribute to the academic and social life of the school. Leaders and teachers encourage families to be strong partners in their children's learning. In addition, leaders and teachers build and sustain partnerships with community organizations and cultural institutions. Students are accustomed to interacting with visiting community members.

A. Welcoming Families and Visitors

1. Leaders and teachers offer a variety of ways for families to participate in the school community (e.g., as a board member, Leadership Team member, tutor, reading buddy, classroom expert, passage portfolio panelist, fundraiser). They seek opportunities to build on and build up parents' strengths as partners in their child's education.

2. Leaders and teachers organize interactive family education events throughout the year (e.g., orientation, an open house to showcase work in progress, a family mathematics night, workshops on social and emotional learning). Such events are opportunities for families to participate as learners and teachers.

3. Leaders and teachers teach students how to actively welcome visitors to the school by training classroom or school ambassadors to welcome guests, share highlights about the school, and speak eloquently about their experience as students.

4. Leaders ensure that student-led tours of the school are tours of learning, not just physical tours to point out the rooms. Students describe the student work on the walls, in portfolios, and in classrooms. They share the story of the school and explain the school's mission and Habits of Character.

B. Building Relationships with Families

1. School leaders and teachers actively seek to learn about the cultures, backgrounds, and values of their students' families. They understand that families from historically underserved groups may have had negative experiences with schooling—their own or their children's. Leaders and teachers work to earn the trust of all families through the following strategies:

    a. Leaders and teachers examine their own biases and personal stories around race, ethnicity, class, gender, and the struggle for educational diversity and equity

within and beyond their community in order to develop empathy for students and families.

   b. Leaders and teachers develop and seek input on school procedures and systems that are inclusive and respectful of all members of the school community and all the ways they can contribute to the school.

   c. Leaders and teachers create structures and traditions to welcome families *throughout* the year, not just at the beginning of the year.

2. Leaders and teachers recognize that families are an important part of the broader crew that supports students to succeed. They demonstrate that they are accessible, visible, and come to the table as learners and partners with families through the following actions:

   a. Leaders articulate clear expectations for families' role and responsibilities in their child's education.

   b. Leaders and teachers provide volunteer opportunities for families.

   c. Leaders articulate grievance procedures that respect families as partners, value all voices, and help all members hold each other accountable for upholding the school's mission and norms.

3. Leaders and teachers encourage and support all families to participate in school events. They schedule events outside of the school day, assist with transportation, provide food, childcare, and translators, and otherwise seek to make school participation accessible and equitable for all families.

4. Leaders create channels to get feedback from families, foster respectful communication, hear diverse perspectives, and facilitate collaborative problem solving when conflicts arise.

5. School leaders systematically and transparently track family participation and feedback through volunteer logs

and school event evaluations. Leaders respond to these data by revising strategies to ensure maximum involvement of families.

C. Communicating with Families

1. Leaders and teachers communicate with families regularly and respectfully before and throughout the school year.

    a. Leaders and teachers create, publicize, and frequently update an annual calendar of events and meetings that invites families to celebrate with students, contribute to the school, and participate in the school's decision-making and planning (e.g., celebrations of learning, community workdays, fund-raisers, school improvement planning).

    b. Leaders develop a publication plan that includes a range of publications and formats (e.g., handbooks, newsletters, annual report, website, e-blast, online grade book) to ensure that all families have access to and understand the school's policies, curriculum, approaches to instruction, and assessment system. They examine and revise the plan to ensure that every family has access, including families whose home language, levels of education, or technological means may present barriers to access.

    c. Leaders and teachers communicate regularly and in a variety of ways with families about students' progress and accomplishments (e.g., informal notes home, interim and end-of-term progress reports, conferences, emails, phone calls).

    d. Leaders seek input from families that don't come to events. They inquire about family members' needs, hopes, and concerns and create ways for all families to participate, including providing translation for families that require it.

2. Leaders and teachers develop protocols and documents to support student-led conferences as a cornerstone of communicating student achievement. (See also *Core Practice 31: Communicating Student Achievement*.) They expect and support all families to participate in this practice. They expect all students to prepare for and do their best in their conference.

3. Leaders and teachers regularly showcase student work and student reflections in schoolwide or classroom-based celebrations of learning. During these events, students themselves act as presenters and docents to explain their learning to families.

D. Building Community Partnerships

1. Leaders and teachers build and sustain relationships with community organizations and cultural institutions that support key school structures like fieldwork, experts, service learning, and authentic audiences for student work.

2. Leaders intentionally build relationships within the community to develop a broad constituency that supports and advocates for the school.

3. Leaders, teachers, and students embrace their responsibility as members of and contributors to the surrounding community.

4. Leaders, teachers, and students recognize the contributions of outside experts and volunteers (e.g., experts are invited to celebrations of learning; students send thank you notes to volunteers).

Core Practice 25

Creating Beautiful Spaces That Promote Learning

In the EL Education model, the physical space of the school reflects and supports the learning environment and the values of the school. When people enter the school, they are immediately aware of being in a place that celebrates learning. The walls are filled with high-quality student work showcased in common spaces and classrooms. Student work is displayed in a way that honors the work, giving parts of the school a museum quality that inspires student and community pride. Work is often supported by explanatory text that includes student voice and reflection. The mission of the school is evident to guests, students, and teachers throughout the building.

Student achievement is honored in public spaces, whether it is academic, artistic, athletic, or a demonstration of good character. Students themselves are leaders in caring for common spaces within the school and on the grounds, helping to make and keep the school as beautiful as possible.

A. Designing the Learning Space

1. School leaders, teachers, and students ensure that classrooms and common spaces are clean and maintained with care and pride. Whenever possible, students are leaders in this work.

2. The primary entryways for the school are welcoming and beautiful, with displays that send a clear message that the school is a place of high achievement, quality work, and student and adult character. Signage makes the values and mission of the school clear to all.

3. Leaders and teachers display high-quality student work rather than commercial posters and signs in classrooms and common spaces. Student work is supported with text that makes clear what students learned. Often, students also create signs related to the school's values, Habits of Character, or norms.

4. Teachers design classroom spaces that are rich with resources for student learning (e.g., books, technology, manipulatives, art supplies, science equipment, models, natural specimens).

5. Teachers design classrooms to facilitate student thinking, independence, and character development. They organize and label supplies, post expectations, directions, and schedules, and artistically display current academic work as well as anchor charts representing key learning.

6. Students take primary responsibility for the care of classroom resources. They treat the learning environment, in particular live plants and animals, with great respect and care.

7. Throughout the building, leaders and teachers celebrate and visibly showcase work that references EL Education's Dimensions of Student Achievement: mastery of knowledge and skills, character, and high-quality student work. They display tributes to sportsmanship, adventure learning, art, and other academic pursuits.

8. Teachers and students connect their classroom learning to the natural world by caring for and learning in outdoor spaces. Often, they display items from the natural world (e.g., plants, rocks and minerals, bones, aquariums and terrariums with live animals) as they would be displayed in a museum, in order to inspire wonder and scientific understanding.

B. Documenting Student Learning

1. Teachers and students create artful displays of student work that feature the work of all students, honoring individual and collective growth and inspiring all students to create work of quality.

2. Teachers and students use bulletin boards and hallway walls to tell the story of student learning through documentation panels that include artifacts such as:

   a. Rough and final draft student work

   b. Guiding questions and learning targets

   c. A narrative about the learning

   d. Photographs

   e. Quotes from students and teachers

   f. Student and teacher reflections

3. Students' presentations of their learning, referencing documentation panels, are a highlight of celebrations of learning.

Core Practice 26

Promoting Courage and Adventure

The spirit of courage and adventure that permeates the EL Education model is a clear expression of EL Education's roots in Outward Bound. Leaders and teachers encourage students to work on building their courage across multiple aspects of their academic and social lives, to develop, for example, "fractions courage," "poetry courage," or "friendship courage." Similarly, adventure can be any physical, artistic, or academic experience that involves risk, challenge, and discovery. Adventure bolsters student engagement and strengthens students' courage.

EL Education promotes the kinds of adventures that create opportunities for leadership and collaboration as groups of students and teachers face challenges both alone and together. Reflection is a vital component of such adventures, so that each experience is a rich opportunity for learning about oneself, one's peers, and the world. Teachers take care when planning adventures to ensure physical and emotional safety, while at the same time promoting risk-taking and courageous action.

A. Learning through Adventure

1. Leaders and teachers build community and provide opportunities for student leadership and teamwork through school adventure traditions. These traditions scaffold through increasingly challenging physical and academic adventures (e.g., a first-grade campout in the gym, a sixth-grade bike trip, a ninth-grade mural project, a high school service project).

2. Leaders and teachers sometimes facilitate outdoor adventures in which students investigate the natural world in open spaces near the school, local parks, or through school-organized wilderness and nature experiences. Leaders and teachers offer outdoor adventure opportunities with the following features:

    a. Leaders and teachers ensure that such adventure experiences are accessible to all students regardless of ability to pay, physical ability, or experience in the outdoors.

    b. Leaders and teachers challenge students to stretch their comfort zones, work together to accomplish a difficult goal, and gain confidence in their individual skills in the face of challenge.

    c. Teachers embrace their own challenges and model healthy risk-taking. They learn and grow alongside their students.

3. Leaders and teachers structure multiple opportunities for students to reflect on and learn from successes and challenges in their physical and academic adventures. They circle up and debrief frequently, focusing on topics such as healthy risk-taking, collaboration and leadership strategies, and how the culture of crew supports individuals to do more than they think possible.

4. Teachers explicitly frame challenging tasks in lessons, case studies, projects, and learning expeditions as opportunities for academic courage, grappling, and risk-taking. Students embrace academic courage through challenge in the classroom.

5. Teachers help students to identify new challenges as learners and to choose tasks that are both meaningful and challenging, such as conducting original research, collaborating with professionals, and revising products multiple times for authentic audiences.

6. Leaders and teachers craft experiences and debriefs that help students understand that taking risks—with support— is often when the most powerful learning takes place.

    a. Teachers promote fieldwork in the natural world or in a city environment as an opportunity to embrace courage and adventure.

    b. Teachers frame student leadership roles (e.g., peer mediation groups, mentoring younger students) as opportunities to embrace courage and adventure.

    c. Leaders promote collaborations between schools or between their school and a local nonprofit with different context (e.g., pen pal relationships with a school in another country, a joint service project between students in different neighborhoods) as opportunities to embrace courage and adventure.

7. Leaders and teachers explicitly connect the school's Habits of Character to academic and physical adventure experiences (including individual and team sports) through the following actions:

    a. Supporting students to reflect on their success, challenges, and personal growth on such Habits of Character as perseverance, problem solving, and collaboration

b. Providing constructive feedback to students who take risks and encouraging them to learn from mistakes, rely on their Crew, keep trying, and celebrate small victories as they work toward their goals

c. Celebrating and publicly acknowledging students' courage and growth as the path toward achievement and meeting personal goals

8. Students use reflections from adventure experiences as artifacts or evidence in student portfolios, passage presentations, or other documentation of growth in Habits of Character.

B. Teaching Adventure Skills and Ensuring Safety

1. The school has policies, protocols, and regulations to ensure that physical education classes, sports programs, physical adventure programming, extracurricular programs, and fieldwork are safe. For off-campus adventure programming, they may contract with a professional organization like Outward Bound.

2. Leaders provide professional learning and ongoing coaching to ensure that teachers, Crew leaders, and adventure trip chaperones have the structures and skills to guide adventure activities. Professional learning includes:

a. Developing norms and expectations for collaboration, conflict resolution, monitoring safety, and supporting all students to do more than they think possible

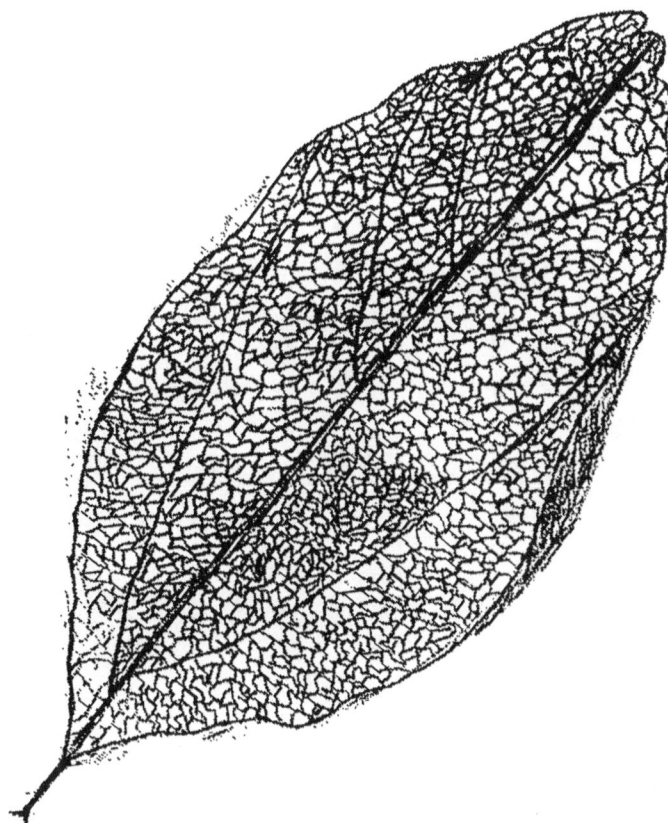

b. Aligning adventure activities with the school's Habits of Character to help teachers and students understand their purpose and value through appropriate framing, implementation, and debrief

c. Giving teachers opportunities to experience and reflect on their own adventure activities and to practice framing and leading adventure-based activities with other adults before they do so with students

d. Training in social and emotional safety (e.g., communication, countering implicit bias, when to defer to professional counselors or therapists)

e. Training in first aid and protocols for emergency situations (e.g., CPR, Wilderness First Aid or Wilderness First Responder medical certifications)

Student-Engaged Assessment

EL Education believes that assessment practices should motivate students to become leaders of their own learning. Students track their progress toward standards-based learning targets, set goals, and reflect on growth and challenges. Students and teachers regularly analyze quantitative and qualitative data that include assessments, reflections, and student work and use those data to inform goals and instruction. Students regularly present evidence of their achievement and growth through student-led family conferences, passage presentations, and celebrations of learning.

Core Practices in This Domain

- Cultivating a Culture of Engagement and Achievement
- Crafting and Using Learning Targets
- Checking for Understanding in Daily Instruction
- Using Assessments to Boost Student Achievement
- Communicating Student Achievement

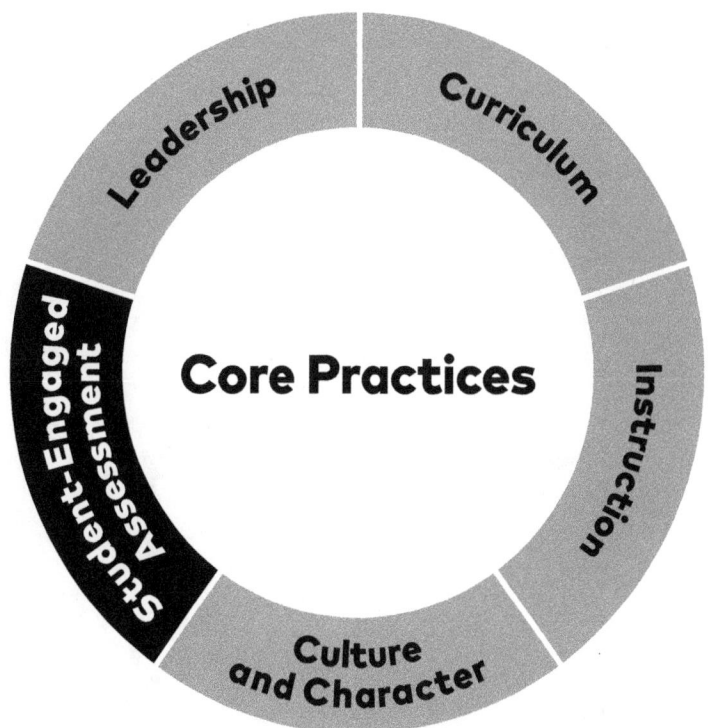

Core Practice 27

Cultivating a Culture of Engagement and Achievement

Student-engaged assessment is a hallmark of the EL Education model. When assessment is done *with* students instead of *to* them, students take responsibility for and lead their own learning. They see themselves as the key actors in their own success. This creates a culture of engagement and achievement in which all students and adults believe that effort and reflection lead to academic growth and high-quality work. Teachers use multiple methods of formative and summative assessment to track students' progress toward academic learning targets and Habits of Scholarship (e.g., perseverance, collaboration, responsibility). Teachers continually analyze quantitative and qualitative evidence of student performance to inform their instruction. Students learn to reflect deeply and concretely on their own performance data, assess their own learning, use feedback from peers and teachers, and set goals for achievement.

A. Developing a Growth Mindset

1. Leaders, teachers, staff, and parents believe and communicate that all students are capable of high academic achievement and that achievement grows with effort. This belief permeates actions and decisions.

   a. Leaders and teachers reinforce their own and students' growth mindset by framing challenging tasks as worthy tasks requiring academic courage and effort.

   b. Leaders provide professional learning for teachers and education for parents on the impact of academic mindsets on achievement.

   c. Leaders and teachers examine assessment practices for implicit bias toward historically underserved groups.

2. Teachers recognize and reinforce students' effort, perseverance, and strategic actions. They avoid "fixed mindset" comments about ability, intelligence, or talent.

3. Teachers and students provide descriptive feedback that empowers students and peers to build on their strengths, learn from mistakes, revise, and correct misconceptions.

B. Supporting Students to Be Leaders of Their Own Learning

1. Teachers translate required standards and Habits of Scholarship into academic and character learning targets for lessons, projects, units, and courses. (See also *Core Practice 28: Crafting and Using Learning Targets.*)

2. Teachers use learning targets purposefully to ensure that students take ownership of their own learning.

3. Teachers provide opportunities for students to reflect on and analyze data as a way to track progress toward learning targets and set goals. (See also *Core Practice 30: Using Assessments to Boost Student Achievement.*)

   a. Students use data from checks for understanding, written formative assessments, interim assessments, or summative assessments (e.g., patterns of error on a math test, time spent on homework) to analyze the root cause of successes and challenges in meeting specific learning targets.

   b. Students regularly assess their own growth through organizing and reflecting on evidence of their learning They are required and supported to present their work publicly and share their analysis and goals.

4. Teachers guide students to assess and improve the quality of their work through the use of models, critique, rubrics, and, sometimes, work with experts. (See also *Core Practice 12: Planning for and Supporting High-Quality Work.*)

5. Teachers articulate how assessments are a source of information that helps students grow. Incremental successes motivate students to step up to increasing levels of challenge.

Core Practice 28
Crafting and Using Learning Targets

Learning targets are the foundation of a student-engaged assessment system. Teachers translate required standards into learning goals for courses, projects, units, and lessons in language that students can understand and own. Teachers refer continually to learning targets during the lesson, check for understanding of learning targets, construct formative and summative assessments that match learning targets, and track students' progress toward targets. Students demonstrate their ownership of their learning by articulating the connections between learning targets and the work of the lesson and by showing evidence of their progress toward meeting them.

A. Crafting Learning Targets

1. Teachers analyze their curriculum map. (See also *Core Practice 2: Mapping Knowledge, Skills, and Habits of Character*.) They unpack and discuss their standards with grade-level peers to develop a deep and shared understanding of what the standards are asking students to know and do.

2. Teachers analyze and discuss the discipline-specific ways of thinking expected by the standards for their subject area (e.g., classifying in science, valuing evidence in ELA, abstract reasoning in math) and can articulate how these ways of thinking support learning.

3. Teachers document and periodically review the alignment of standards, learning targets, and assessments as part of their curriculum maps.

4. Teachers translate their standards into high-quality learning targets that have the following characteristics:

   a. They are derived from national or state standards embedded in school or district documents such as curriculum maps and adopted program materials.

   b. They are written in student-friendly language and begin with the stem "I can...."

   c. They are measurable and use concrete, assessable verbs (e.g., identify, compare, analyze).

   d. They are specific, often referring to the particular context of a lesson, project, or case study.

   e. They are phrased to identify the intended learning, not the intended doing. That is, learning targets are phrased as statements about the skills or knowledge students will develop as opposed to what students will complete (e.g., "I can describe the ideal habitat for a polar bear" vs. "I can write a paragraph about the habitat of a polar bear").

   f. They are phrased to identify the knowledge, reasoning, or skill that matches the cognitive process demanded of students (e.g., "analyzing" or "creating").

5. Teachers sequence daily learning targets that scaffold students' ability to achieve mastery of a standard. When sequencing targets, teachers consider the following questions:

   a. How many lessons do students need to master the discrete skill, knowledge, or reasoning in this learning target?

   b. What sequence of daily learning targets will build students' knowledge and skills over time, scaffolding students to mastery of a standard (or long-term target)?

   c. What character learning targets support the topic and tasks I'm asking students to do (e.g., "I can seek multiple perspectives in our discussion of civil rights," "I can persevere to improve my work through multiple revisions")?

   d. When should I use a character learning target alongside an academic target so that students have multiple opportunities for growth (e.g., "I can be productive and focused when working independently," "I can contribute to my classroom community by reliably doing my classroom job," "I can speak and listen respectfully to my peers")?

B. Using Learning Targets in Daily Instruction

1. Teachers use learning targets to articulate specific learning outcomes for students, so that all students know the target they are aiming for and understand the criteria for success before independent practice. Teachers unpack the learning target with students through the following actions:

   a. Guiding students to restate the learning target verb in their own words (e.g., analyze, explain, solve)

   b. Identifying and defining academic or domain-specific vocabulary in the learning target

   c. Communicating how the learning target will be assessed before students demonstrate their learning in relation to the target

2. Teachers sometimes pre-assess students' proficiency on the learning target as part of the "do now" activity in a lesson.

3. Teachers choose the optimal time to introduce learning targets during a lesson. (See also *Core Practice 10: Planning Effective Lessons* and *Core Practice 11: Delivering Effective Lessons*.)

   a. In a Workshop 1.0 lesson, this is typically at the outset of the lesson, or after a "hook" that builds excitement.

   b. For a discovery-based lesson or Workshop 2.0 lesson structure, this is typically after students have grappled with a problem or text, discussed their strategies, or raised questions and hypotheses.

4. Teachers refer to the learning target throughout the lesson through the following actions:

   a. Explaining how daily learning targets are related to standards or long-term learning targets

   b. Pausing instruction or work time periodically to reorient students to the learning target and correct misconceptions or false starts

   c. Using checks for understanding to assess where students are in relation to the learning target

   d. Debriefing the learning in the context of the learning target at the end of the lesson

5. Teachers ensure that students:

   a. Can articulate the meaning and purpose of learning targets

   b. Regularly track their progress toward learning targets through quick checks, formative assessments, or target trackers

   c. Know where they are in relation to the learning target and what they need to do to get closer to meeting it

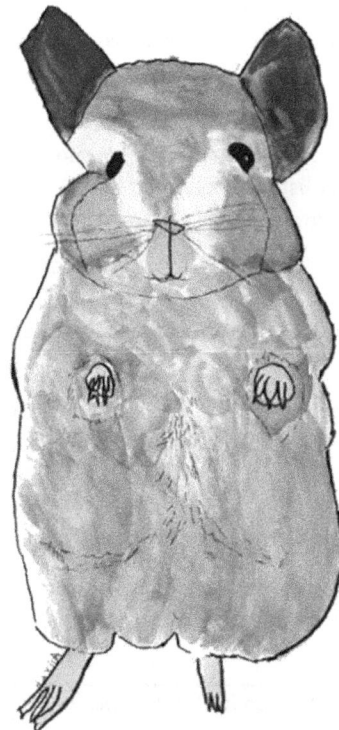

Core Practice 29
Checking for Understanding in Daily Instruction

The EL Education model promotes student-engaged assessment strategies that help students reflect on and lead their own learning. Teachers use these strategies so that students understand what they know and can do at the outset of learning and as they progress toward learning targets. Students are able to articulate their understanding and set meaningful goals for applying their learning and improving their work.

A. Starting with Learning Targets[5]

1. Teachers anchor their planning, lessons, and assessments in well-crafted learning targets.

2. Teachers gauge student progress against learning targets. They ensure that students know and can articulate where they are in relation to proficiency on academic and character learning targets.

B. Using Protocols and Engagement Strategies

1. Teachers use protocols and engagement strategies to ensure that all students participate in whole group discussions (e.g., Cold Call, No Opt Out).

2. Teachers engage students actively and equitably (e.g., by using Think-Pair-Share, Back-to-Back and Face-to-Face).

3. Teachers use Conversation Cues that promote productive and collaborative discussion (e.g., "Tell me more," "How is what x said different than what y said?").

C. Listening and Observing Strategically

1. Teachers circulate while students are working and engaged in structured small-group discussions to observe learning in action (e.g., during the "grapple" portion of a Workshop 2.0 lesson, they listen to determine what students collectively know or can do and to identify common misconceptions).

2. During observation, teachers ask open-ended (how? why? what if?) questions that prompt students to extend their thinking.

3. Teachers sometimes use a checklist to track evidence as they circulate, especially during the "apply" portion of a Workshop 2.0 lesson.

D. Using Quick-Check Techniques

1. Teachers use quick-check techniques to engage students in checking their own understanding, to monitor confusion or readiness, to determine the status of the class as a whole, or to probe for deeper understanding (e.g., Go Around, Clickers, Human Bar Graph, Hot Seat).

2. Teachers periodically pause instruction or work time to address misconceptions or false starts.

E. Deepening Understanding through Questioning

1. Teachers ask sequenced, pre-planned strategic questions that deepen critical thinking and build students' understanding of the concept or skill in the lesson.

2. Teachers require students to use evidence from the text or data sets to support their answers.

3. Teachers help students learn how to formulate their own strategic questions.

4. Teachers encourage students to ask questions of themselves and others to monitor and augment their understanding, especially during the discussion portion of a Workshop 2.0 lesson. (See also *Core Practice 11: Delivering Effective Lessons.*)

5. Teachers provide adequate think time so that all students have time to process and construct an answer.

F. Self-Assessing, Reflecting on Progress, and Setting Goals

1. Teachers use models and critique sessions to help students develop an understanding of quality in texts and in their own product creations and to set goals for progress. (See also *Core Practice 12: Planning for and Supporting High-Quality Student Work.*)

2. Teachers provide descriptive feedback and facilitate peer feedback sessions that enable students to reflect, self-assess, and set goals for revision. (See also *Core Practice 12: Planning for and Supporting High-Quality Student Work.*)

---

5. This practice is detailed in *Core Practice 28: Crafting and Using Learning Targets.*

3. Teachers debrief lessons to help students reflect on their individual and collective progress. Students reflect on both what they learned and how they learned, using private and public protocols for reflection (e.g., journals, learning target trackers, exit tickets, or dialogue).

4. Teachers provide explicit instruction on self-assessing with accuracy (e.g., with reference to specific criteria lists or rubrics) and providing evidence to support their claims about progress toward learning targets.

5. Teachers help students identify strategies and next steps needed to achieve learning targets. With support from teachers, students create action plans for academic goals as well as Habits of Character.

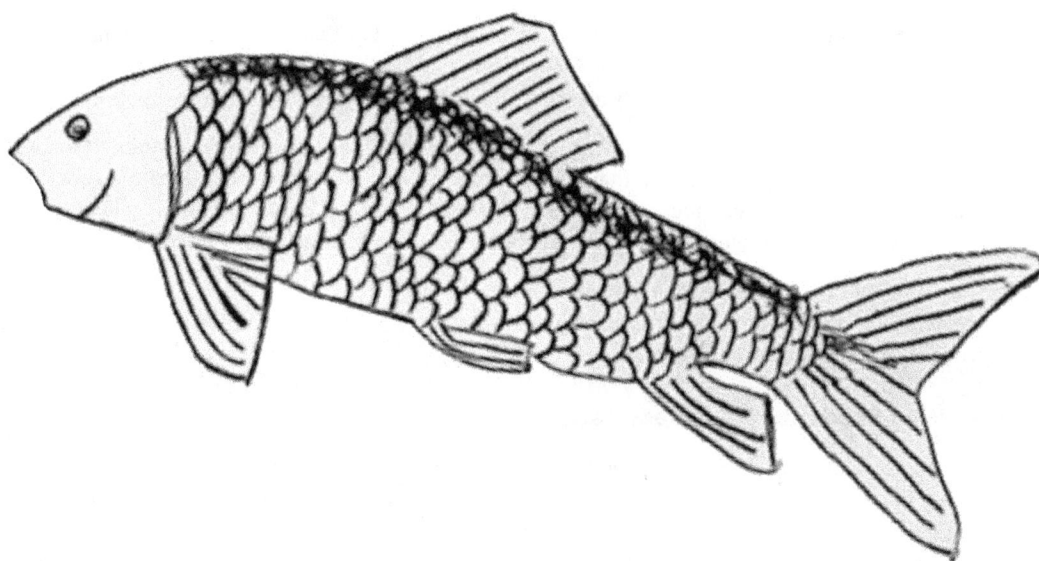

Core Practice 30

Using Assessments to Boost Student Achievement

In the EL Education model, teachers and leaders use a variety of assessment types to measure students' mastery of standards and regularly involve students in understanding and analyzing their own assessment data. (See also *Core Practice 29: Checking for Understanding in Daily Instruction.*) Teachers use high-quality assessment data, both formative and summative, to reflect on the effectiveness of curriculum, instruction, and schoolwide structures such as schedules, academic groupings, and intervention programs. Finally, assessments provide a body of evidence for grading, reporting, promotion, and graduation that must be communicated to the community, district, state, and other stakeholders.

Teachers and leaders choose, create, and schedule high-quality classroom assessments in order to get a complete and accurate picture of student learning throughout the year and to prepare students for interim assessments and high-stakes standardized tests. They analyze test results to inform action plans, make instructional adjustments, and set goals for improvement. Students also analyze their own data, use it to identify strategies for success, and communicate their data and their goals to families.

A. Choosing or Creating Quality Assessments

1. Teachers choose, adopt, or craft quality assessments in order to collect meaningful, accurate, and timely information about student learning. These include formative and summative assessments (e.g., paper and pencil tests, on-demand assessments of writing, performance assessment tasks, online interim assessments).

2. Teachers align assessments with required standards and then plan backward to identify the sequence of assessments that will be used to measure mastery of concepts and skills incrementally and repeatedly throughout the year.

3. Teachers choose or design and then test-drive major assessments as part of their initial planning for a unit to ensure that these assessments accurately measure and align with desired learning targets.

4. Teachers select the type of assessment that is best matched to what they are assessing (e.g., multiple choice to assess factual knowledge, performance tasks to assess skills).

5. Teachers collaboratively create or choose common assessments for key skills or content. Common assessments improve consistency and reporting of student proficiency.

B. Preparing Students for Assessments

1. Teachers ensure that students understand the purpose and outcomes of different types of assessment so that students clearly see the connection between learning targets and assessments.

2. Teachers scaffold instruction to build students' knowledge, skills, and reasoning (e.g., cognitive strategies such as analysis, interpretation, problem solving). They support students to identify patterns and big ideas linked to disciplinary content.

3. Teachers use formative assessments (assessments for learning) to give students experience with summative assessment tasks (assessments of learning) and build their capacity to accurately self-assess their progress toward learning targets.

4. Teachers encourage productive study habits (e.g., forming peer study groups, text-coding notes, memorizing mnemonics, using flashcards).

5. Teachers prepare students for standardized tests throughout the school year, not as an isolated event just prior to a testing situation.

   a. Teachers help students analyze the formats used on standardized tests (e.g., writing to prompts, multiple choice questions, showing thinking in mathematics and science) and teach them to respond to these formats by applying strategies such as using context clues.

   b. Teachers give strategic practice tests to boost students' confidence with the test-taking format, timing, and procedures.

   c. Teachers empower students to improve their performance by applying test-taking strategies, strengthening Habits of Scholarship (e.g., time management, perseverance, problem solving), and practicing self-care to reduce test anxiety (e.g., exercise, a healthy diet, sleep, meditation).

C. Using Assessment Data with Students

1. Teachers ensure that related learning targets are posted on assignments, and when appropriate, on assessments, so that students understand how academic tasks demonstrate mastery of targets.

2. Teachers support students to analyze their own assessment data and track their progress toward learning targets. (See also *Core Practice 27: Cultivating a Culture of Engagement and Achievement.*)

3. Students regularly analyze strengths, challenges, and patterns in their performance on assessments and on related assignments. They may keep data notebooks or folders to document their findings.

4. Based on assessment data, students set learning goals and determine next steps to reach them.

5. Students present and explain their own data to families in student-led conferences. (See also *Core Practice 31: Communicating Student Achievement.*)

D. Using Assessment Data to Drive Student Achievement and School Improvement

1. Teachers individually and collaboratively analyze assessment data. They deliberately and thoughtfully use assessment data to identify patterns in student responses to test items. This practice informs curriculum mapping and lesson planning and helps teachers to evaluate, adjust, and differentiate instruction.

2. School leaders provide professional development to support teachers in implementing and analyzing assessments. (See also *Core Practice 33: Leading Evidence-Based Strategic Improvement* and *Core Practice 36: Leading Professional Learning.*)

3. Teachers and school leaders create or select interim assessments, designed to benchmark student progress toward end-of-year goals, that are closely aligned to required standards and standardized tests. They ensure that interim assessments match the rigor of the end-of-year or end-of-course assessments.

4. Leaders and teachers articulate the value and purpose of standardized tests. They help families and students understand that this data allows educators to adjust curriculum and instruction to meet the needs of all students as they move up through the grades.

5. Leaders and leadership teams regularly analyze data as part of the school-improvement process. They use it to set goals and create action plans for improvement and to document growth and achievement.

Core Practice 31
Communicating Student Achievement

In the EL Education model, student achievement is communicated in traditional ways (e.g., report cards) and also in ways that allow students to take the lead in speaking about their own learning. Leaders and teachers create structures and procedures that support students to create, maintain, and present portfolios demonstrating growth and achievement during student-led conferences, passage presentations, and celebrations of learning. They also implement standards-based grading systems that communicate academic outcomes relative to specific required standards and, separately, outcomes on Habits of Scholarship. Teachers involve students in the dialogue about assessment and communicating achievement. Students can articulate what they have learned and speak to their own strengths, struggles, goals, processes of learning, and preparation for college and career success.

A. Implementing Standards-Based Grading

1. Teachers determine grades that describe students' current proficiency in relation to specific standards. For example, they may use a 1–4 point scale, with a 1 meaning a student "does not meet the standard" and a 4 meaning a student "exceeds the standard." Recent evidence takes precedence over older evidence so that students' grades reflect what students know and can do now, rather than an average of their proficiency over time (as represented by a percentage).

2. Teachers within subject-area departments or grade levels compare and calibrate their grading practices to ensure that they are using grades to objectively describe students' mastery of knowledge and skills, not to motivate future efforts or punish past failures.

3. Teachers communicate long-term learning targets to students and families at the outset of instruction. Over the course of the term, they provide students with multiple opportunities to demonstrate progress toward long-term learning targets. Students can articulate how their grades reflect proficiency on learning targets, rather than the subjective judgments of teachers.

4. Leaders and teachers develop uniform grading practices that ensure schoolwide consistency in grading. They communicate these practices to students and families in school documents and timely electronic and verbal communications.

5. Teachers determine grades for academic learning targets separate from scores for Habits of Scholarship. Success in both areas is considered in credit, promotion, and graduation policies.

B. Communicating about Habits of Scholarship

1. Leaders and teachers collaborate to create a coherent and consistent system for collecting evidence of students' Habits of Scholarship.

   a. Teachers assess Habits of Scholarship (e.g., perseverance, collaboration).

   b. Teachers often use evidence of homework completion, meeting deadlines, and prompt attendance to support Habits of Scholarship grades.

   c. Teachers and leaders develop rubrics and guidance documents to ensure that all teachers assess Habits of Scholarship fairly and consistently.

2. Leaders and teachers support students and family members to recognize the relationship between Habits of Scholarship and academic achievement.

   a. Leaders, teachers, and students track this correlation over time and share it with families.

   b. Students set goals and write action plans to improve their Habits of Scholarship in order to improve their academic achievement.

3. Teachers report student proficiency on Habits of Scholarship in multiple ways.

   a. Habits of Scholarship are communicated on progress reports (separately from academic grades).

   b. Students provide evidence of and share their progress on Habits of Scholarship in student led-conferences and passage presentations.

   c. Leaders and teachers recognize Habits of Scholarship in school awards, community circles, and other public acknowledgements.

C. Communicating Achievement on Report Cards and Transcripts

1. Teachers report progress toward specific standards-aligned learning targets (not just letter grades).

2. Leaders and teachers ensure that students and families understand the connection between classroom grading policies and school reporting practices.

a. This information is included in family handbooks and family education/information sessions.

b. Teachers often ask students to track and record their own progress toward meeting learning targets during class time. Grades reported at the end of term should not be a surprise to students.

c. Teachers communicate concerns about student progress to students and families along the way, so that students, families, and teachers can intervene appropriately.

3. Leaders create a succinct document that explains how student grades are derived and what they mean. This document accompanies student transcripts when they are sent to outside audiences (e.g., college admissions offices).

D. Communicating Achievement through Celebrations of Learning

1. Leaders and teachers organize grade-level or schoolwide events to celebrate the learning of all students. These often take place at the end of learning expeditions, units, or school terms.

2. Teachers invite families, community members, and school partners to serve as an authentic audience for celebrations of learning.

3. Teachers prepare students to serve as docents and presenters of their own learning and create protocols that enable family members to ask questions about student work, interact with students and teachers, and honor the school's mission.

E. Communicating Achievement through Portfolios

1. Leaders and teachers collaborate to create a system for documenting student work across subject areas in portfolios.

   a. Teachers define the purpose and organizing structure of portfolios (e.g., by discipline, dimension of achievement, or learning target).

   b. Teachers determine what will be in portfolios to provide context for student work (e.g., a table of contents, reflections, resume, section overviews, assignment rubrics showing learning targets).

   c. Teachers determine what student work will be included, how pieces will be selected, and whether to include multiple drafts, self-reflections, or feedback from teachers. They create a checklist or other guidance documents to help students create quality portfolios for presentation.

   d. Teachers determine whether to include service learning logs and/or reflections on Habits of Character.

F. Communicating Achievement through Student-Led Conferences

1. Leaders schedule time at least twice per year for student-led conferences in which students communicate progress in their learning to family members or other caregivers. Student-led conferences address all EL Education's Dimensions of Student Achievement: mastery of knowledge and skills, character, and high-quality student work.

2. Leaders and teachers support families to understand the structure, purpose, and expectations of student-led conferences. They communicate the schedule in advance and help families understand the roles and responsibilities of teachers, students, and parents during the conference.

3. Teachers or Crew leaders support students in preparing for conferences (often during Crew) by doing the following:

   a. Creating classroom systems for archiving student work

   b. Supporting students in selecting work for their portfolios

   c. Supporting students in naming and being able to demonstrate what they have learned

   d. Supporting students to reflect on and articulate their progress, to identify areas for growth, and to set aspirational and achievable goals

   e. Making time for students to prepare for and practice their student-led conference presentation, with attention to criteria such as eye contact, clear articulation, and presenting evidence to support their claims about learning

G. Communicating Achievement through Passage Presentations

1. Leaders and teachers create passage presentation structures in which students present their readiness to move forward to the next level of their educational journey (e.g., from elementary to middle school, middle to high school, high school to college).

2. Leaders and teachers determine the purpose and objectives of passage presentations. Depending on the grade level of the passage and the school's mission, they identify what students will focus on in their presentation (e.g., work that demonstrates proficiency in core subjects; artistic, athletic, or technical accomplishments; service and leadership; growth in Habits of Character).

3. Teachers and leaders formulate a rubric and other guidance documents that convey the vision of student success in a passage presentation through the following actions:

Communicating Student Achievement (continued)

   a. Determining whom the authentic audience for passage presentations will include (e.g., community members, board members, Crew mates)

   b. Determining how passage presentations will be structured and what will be assessed

   c. Determining how and when students will prepare for passage presentations and how information will be communicated to families

4. Teachers support students to prepare for passage presentations well in advance of the event (often during Crew) by doing the following:

   a. Supporting students to analyze their own portfolios and to identify quality evidence that demonstrates progress toward academic and character learning targets and readiness for passage

   b. Helping students select and reflect on student work to showcase in their passage presentation

   c. Making time for students to practice and receive feedback on presentation skills such as eye contact, effective communication of ideas, use of technology, and presenting evidence to support their statements

Leadership

EL Education supports school leaders to build a cohesive school vision focused on EL Education's Three Dimensions of Student Achievement, continuous improvement, and shared leadership. They align resources and activities to the school's vision and lead a professional culture with a growth mindset. Leaders shape school structures to provide equitable education to all students, celebrate joy in learning, and build a schoolwide learning community of trust and collaboration. Leaders work collaboratively with families, staff, and students to make evidence-based decisions that enable all students to achieve.

Note: "School leaders" in this section refers to principals, instructional coaches and guides, and teachers in leadership roles. "Administrative leaders" refers specifically to principals or leaders in executive or supervisory roles.

Core Practices in This Domain

- Fostering a Cohesive School Vision
- Leading Evidence-Based Strategic Improvement
- Cultivating a Positive Professional Culture
- Promoting Shared Leadership
- Leading Professional Learning
- Ensuring High-Quality Instruction

Core Practice 32

Fostering a Cohesive School Vision

In the EL Education model, leaders unite staff, students, and the broader community around an inspirational vision of student success rooted in EL Education's Dimensions of Student Achievement: mastery of knowledge and skills, character, and high-quality student work. This vision transforms schools into places where students and adults engage in purposeful, challenging, and joyful learning. School leaders align resources to support all domains of the school—Curriculum, Instruction, Culture and Character, Student-Engaged Assessment, and Leadership—to this vision.

Note: "School leaders" in this section refers to principals, instructional coaches and guides, and teachers in leadership roles. "Administrative leaders" refers specifically to principals or leaders in executive or supervisory roles.

A. Creating and Aligning a Cohesive School Vision

1. School leaders engage multiple stakeholders in co-creating a shared vision for school success centered on challenging, engaging, and empowering all students. They develop a clear vision for what a graduate of their school will know and be able to do and the high-quality teaching and learning that will produce these outcomes. They ensure that student achievement across EL Education's Dimensions of Student Achievement lives at the heart of the vision.

2. School leaders articulate an explicit and firm commitment to ensuring equally high learning outcomes for all students regardless of background or identity (e.g., race, gender, socioeconomic status, linguistic heritage, physical or learning ability, immigrant status, religion, culture).

3. School leaders align all curriculum, policies, management structures, resources, decision-making processes, and other leadership actions to the vision.

B. Communicating and Engaging Others in the Vision

1. School leaders articulate how implementing EL Education Core Practices helps the school achieve its vision. They champion a school in which teachers can fulfill their highest aspirations and students can achieve more than they think possible.

2. School leaders continuously promote the vision to all stakeholders by communicating the characteristics of a graduate and why they are important. This includes the following actions:

   a. Articulating the vision to stakeholders in the course of formal and informal interactions

   b. Promoting the vision through family handbooks, faculty handbooks, the school website, social media, regular communications to staff and families, annual reports, and other communications for a variety of audiences

   c. Ensuring that the physical design of the school environment, including banners and informational displays in the school building and grounds, promotes the vision

3. School leaders work together with teachers and families to communicate to students the school's vision. Students can articulate their role as stewards of this vision.

4. School leaders inspire and amplify the enthusiasm and expertise of staff, families, and members of the community toward the shared vision. They give credit to others and celebrate the spirit and work of the school community in fulfilling the vision.

C. Aligning Human Capital to Fulfill the Vision

1. School leaders strategically define the roles and responsibilities of staff.

   a. Administrative leaders identify the professional knowledge and skills necessary to achieve the vision. They articulate and periodically revise job descriptions for all positions in the school.

   b. Administrative leaders allocate staff tactically and flexibly; they don't make assignments based simply on what's always been done. They analyze data to understand student learning needs and match responsibilities to roles so that workloads maximize impact on student learning and are equitable and manageable.

   c. Administrative leaders communicate supervisory relationships clearly through staffing models, organizational charts, and handbooks.

2. Administrative leaders recruit and hire staff to support the vision.

   a. Administrative leaders proactively recruit within and beyond the traditional applicant pool to select teachers whose practice and experience are aligned with the school's vision and the EL Education model.

b. Administrative leaders recruit and select teachers who:

    i. Have experience or demonstrated commitment to raising student achievement; a belief in every student's capacity for leadership, critical thinking, and service; and the ability to form strong relationships with students and their families

    ii. View the cultural and linguistic backgrounds of their students as assets for teaching and learning and are committed to increasing their cultural proficiency in working with students from backgrounds different from their own

    iii. Are committed to professional learning, collaborative planning, and the common vision and mission of the school

3. Administrative leaders use clear protocols and processes in hiring. They involve other faculty members (and sometimes students, families and/ or community partners) through hiring committees, group interview processes, and other structures.

4. Administrative leaders require finalists for teaching positions to demonstrate their teaching proficiency (e.g., presenting sample curricula, facilitating a lesson with students or adults, sharing a portfolio of prior teaching experience).

D. Aligning Calendars and Schedules to Fulfill the Vision

1. School leaders design a yearlong calendar that maximizes learning time for both students and adults, as well as time for school events and traditions.

2. School leaders plan for significant professional learning required to implement or improve educational practices, including full professional learning days and/or summer institutes.

3. School leaders schedule opportunities for family engagement and participation in school traditions, leadership, and service. When scheduling events, school leaders are mindful of families' competing commitments. They strive to disrupt inequities in family involvement through thoughtful scheduling and outreach.

4. When necessary, school leaders advocate boldly and creatively with their district leaders or boards for more control over use of time to allow the EL Education model to be implemented with integrity (e.g., they negotiate exceptions to policies to allow for teacher professional learning, Crew, and student projects).

5. School leaders use the school's daily and weekly schedule as a significant lever for fulfilling the vision. They design a schedule that does the following:

    a. Cultivates a positive school culture by ensuring time for Crew, community meetings, and other culture-building routines

    b. Provides time for individual teacher planning time and common grade-level or subject area planning time, as well as professional learning

    c. Provides dedicated time for whole staff meetings, teacher leadership meetings, and meetings with parents or special education teams

    d. Allows for flexible, uninterrupted blocks of time that foster deeper learning, content-based literacy, project-based learning, fieldwork, and student presentations

    e. Allows for flexible grouping and gives all students access to a challenging, college-ready curriculum

        i. Any grouping for intervention is temporary and does not, by design, limit future opportunities or create differing levels of expectation. Tracking students by ability is not practiced in EL Education schools.

        ii. Exceptional learners, including students identified as academically gifted, students with disabilities, and English language learners, are taught in regular education classrooms to the greatest extent possible.

6. School leaders customize the school schedule to challenge and support all students.

E. Aligning the Budget to Fulfill the Vision

1. Administrative leaders regularly analyze existing budget allocations and make decisions to redistribute, eliminate, and/or expand allocations based on the learning needs of students. Students with the greatest needs receive the most support.

2. Administrative leaders develop budgets that support materials and resources for on-site professional learning and travel and registration costs for off-site learning.

3. School leaders allocate money to support intensive professional learning during school breaks and throughout the year.

4. School leaders allocate money to support the curriculum, including books and materials to support deeper learning.

5. School leaders allocate money to teachers and/or teams to support fieldwork, final products, culminating events, and collaboration with outside experts.

Core Practice 33

Leading Evidence-Based Strategic Improvement

In the EL Education model, school leaders carefully set priorities and then keep their focus squarely on those priorities until they are achieved. To do this, they engage their school community in a strategic improvement process that identifies a limited number of high-priority goals, strategies, and a clear timetable that will guide actions as they work toward the vision. Leaders then deliberately and creatively align available resources (people, time, money) to fulfill the vision.

Note: "School leaders" in this section refers to district leaders, principals, instructional coaches and guides, and teachers in leadership roles. "Administrative leaders" refers specifically to principals or leaders in district, executive, or supervisory roles.

A. Developing a Strategy for Continuous Improvement

1. Administrative leaders partner with EL Education to develop a long-term plan for realizing the school vision through implementation of the EL Education model.

2. School leaders collaborate with EL Education coaches to create long-term goals and annual benchmarks aligned to EL Education's Dimensions of Student Achievement and grounded in baseline data. They make time for regular meetings and check-ins with EL Education coaches.

3. School leaders engage a range of stakeholders in a collaborative process to design a strategy or work plan driven by data analysis. They select a few high-leverage improvement efforts that—if effectively supported—will lead to the greatest amount of growth in student achievement.

4. School leaders align time, resources, and personnel to achieve the priorities included in their work plan. They regularly gather and analyze data that enable them to make minor course corrections as they implement the work plan throughout the school year.

5. Administrative leaders monitor school improvement progress at strategic intervals throughout the year. The strategic improvement cycle includes:

   a. Development of a work plan based on long-term goals and annual priorities

   b. Midyear review of progress toward annual priorities

   c. End-of-year assessment of progress, including completion of the EL Education Implementation Review

   d. Goal-setting and creation of a work plan for the next school year

6. School leaders share the annual priorities and associated work plan with their staff members and other stakeholders. They ensure that staff members understand their roles and responsibilities in meeting the annual priorities.

7. School leaders ensure that all initiatives are aligned with their annual work plan goals and strategies and that annual plans continue to align with long-term goals and benchmarks. They leverage the work plan to decline initiatives that are not connected to agreed-upon goals.

8. School leaders use feedback from EL Education coaches along with other sources of evidence to assess leader and teacher growth and to inform the development of the following year's work plan and school improvement priorities.

9. School leaders selectively archive evidence from EL Education's Dimensions of Student Achievement (mastery of knowledge and skills, character, high-quality student work) in order to identify and assess the impact of implementing EL Education practices on student achievement across all three dimensions.

B. Managing Change throughout the Improvement Process

1. School leaders learn about change management. They reflect on how their own leadership actions and style support staff through the change process.

2. School leaders manage the improvement process proactively. They anticipate challenges and regularly analyze and resolve barriers to change.

3. School leaders seek to understand the dynamics of change by listening deeply and considering the needs and voices of all members of their school community.

4. School leaders regularly assess the professional learning

needs of the faculty and take action to address observed gaps.

5. School leaders regularly assess whether resources for instruction, learning, and operations are adequate and take action to address observed shortages.

6. School leaders ensure that there are clear action plans for change initiatives, with defined roles, responsibilities, and timelines.

C. Using Data to Improve Instruction

1. School leaders establish a clear, consistent, no-blame strategy for using data to analyze student achievement across EL Education's Dimensions of Student Achievement and to address gaps and inequities the data reveal.

2. School leaders develop organizational structures that are consistent with strategies intended to address gaps and inequities.

3. School leaders themselves engage in ongoing data analysis, discussion, and reflection that informs their decisions. They select and analyze data for patterns that provide evidence for claims about student achievement.

4. School leaders provide time and resources for teachers to collaboratively analyze data and to make critical evidence-based decisions.

5. School leaders and teachers monitor data to identify and address patterns of inequity. They take responsibility for increasing the achievement of all students through the following actions:

   a. Disaggregating and examining student achievement by a range of demographic groups, including gender, race, socioeconomic status, language-learner status, and special education status

   b. Looking for patterns of disproportionate representation of any particular group

   c. Examining practice to identify unconscious biases and designing systems to reduce the effects of these biases (e.g., blind grading, choosing students randomly using popsicle sticks, sometimes called "equity sticks")

   d. Identifying short-term interventions to ensure that every student's needs are met

   e. Designing long-term action plans that proactively ensure all students meet or exceed standards and that decrease the need for reactive remediation

6. School leaders support the collection of high-quality evidence from multiple data sources for each of EL Education's Dimensions of Student Achievement. Evidence recommended on the EL Education Implementation Review rubrics includes:

   a. Mastery of knowledge and skills:
      i. School progress reports
      ii. Interim assessments (e.g., NWEA Measures of Academic Performance)
      iii. Standardized tests (local, state, and national)
      iv. Performance or on-demand assessments
      v. Representative collections of student work samples
      vi. Classroom observations
      vii. Postgraduation performance indicators (e.g., college acceptance, college readiness assessments)

   b. Character
      i. Surveys completed by staff or students
      ii. Attendance, attrition, promotion, and graduation records
      iii. Discipline records
      iv. Measures of student engagement and motivation
      v. Summaries of schoolwide Habits of Scholarship/ Habits of Character data
      vi. School climate surveys
      vii. Random and representative classroom and hallway observations

   c. High-Quality Student Work
      i. Expedition products
      ii. Random and representative samples of daily work, project work, student portfolios
      iii. High-Quality Work Protocol summary

7. School leaders select and employ appropriate technology to support data collection and storage so that they have access to data in formats that are easy to interpret, analyze, and act upon.

8. School leaders organize data displays that facilitate analysis by a variety of stakeholders. Data is presented so that it can be analyzed effectively and efficiently.

9. School leaders facilitate evidence-based conversations with teachers, families, students, and other stakeholders to foster inquiry, problem solving, and collective ownership of student success.

10. School leaders make current data available to stakeholder groups in a timely fashion while that data is still relevant and helpful.

11. School leaders use evidence to tell their school's story, spearhead change, and allocate resources.

Leading Evidence-Based Strategic Improvement (continued)

D. Building Staff Capacity for Using Data

1. School leaders invest in the capacity of every teacher to access, understand, and use data effectively. They provide ongoing professional learning focused on analyzing multiple types of data and properly interpreting results.

2. School leaders and teachers share accountability for results in a culture that focuses collaboratively on solutions rather than on placing blame for trends in student achievement.

3. Leaders develop protocols and norms that engage teachers in solution-oriented, evidence-based conversations.

4. Leaders model and hold teachers accountable for using evidence to make decisions about improvements in instruction.

E. Engaging the School Community and Other Stakeholders with Data

1. School leaders facilitate evidence- and data-informed conversations with families and other stakeholders to foster inquiry, problem solving, and collective ownership of student success.

2. School leaders support collection and shared analysis of data about community engagement. They use multiple sources of evidence (e.g., student and family satisfaction surveys, volunteer logs, community attendance at school events).

3. School leaders support the collection and shared analysis of data about organizational performance. They use multiple sources of evidence (e.g., enrollment patterns, budget targets, resources and fundraising, and staff recruitment, retention, and satisfaction).

4. School leaders use data to tell their school's story, spearhead change, and allocate resources. They make current data available to stakeholder groups in a timely fashion while the data are still relevant and helpful.

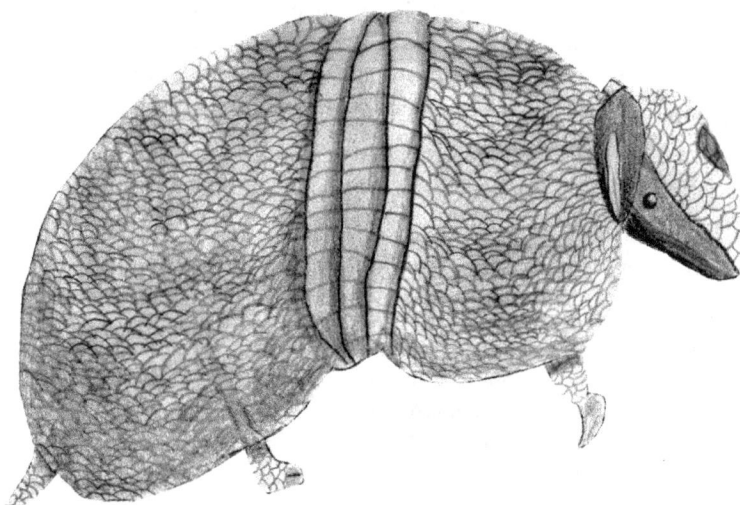

Core Practice 34
Cultivating a Positive Professional Culture

In the EL Education model, leaders cultivate a professional culture among adults that parallels the empowering culture they foster for students. (See also *Core Practice 23: Building the Culture and Structure of Crew*.) School leaders build trust so that educators can take risks, show vulnerability, and explore new practices that lead to increased student achievement. School leaders support this growth-oriented and impact-focused professional collaboration by creating professional communities where adults bring their whole selves to work and where they continually improve their ability to work productively with each other. This means leaders invite and facilitate honest, direct feedback, and, when needed, candid and courageous conversations. They prioritize growth more than the status quo and implement an asset-based orientation toward all members of the school community. School leaders embody the school's values and exemplify the positive and professional character they want all staff to demonstrate. Leaders foster an environment where all staff members feel safe, valued, and productive in a culture that respectfully challenges them to do more than they think possible.

Note: "School leaders" in this section refers to district leaders, principals, instructional coaches and guides, and teachers in leadership roles. "Administrative leaders" refers specifically to principals or leaders in district, executive, or supervisory roles.

A. Promoting Trust

1. School leaders model fair and equitable behaviors toward staff that foster trust among all staff members. Such behaviors include:

   a. Respectfully and genuinely listening to and valuing the opinions of others in the discourse of the school

   b. Demonstrating personal regard for others and acting with awareness of others' sense of vulnerability

   c. Demonstrating competence in executing their formal responsibilities

   d. Speaking and acting with integrity; following through on commitments

2. School leaders model a growth mindset and professional courage by taking risks in public to try new things, listen to different opinions, own their mistakes, and be explicit about their own growth and revision.

3. School leaders and staff deliberately use structures that foster trust among colleagues. (See also *Core Practice 23: Building the Culture and Structure of Crew*.) Actions that foster trust include:

   a. Establishing and following decision-making models

   b. Establishing norms and reflecting on them regularly

   c. Using protocols to ensure that all voices are heard

   d. Holding space for concerns, questions, and disagreement

   e. Creating and following meeting agendas

   f. Documenting and following up on decisions

4. School leaders share ownership of successes, challenges, and change initiatives. They recognize and appreciate all members of the school community as important actors in the work of improving the school.

B. Establishing a Growth-Oriented Professional Culture

1. School leaders cultivate a culture in which all members of the school community embrace continuous learning and constructive feedback as an investment in their own and the school's success.

2. School leaders use formal structures (e.g., surveys) and informal conversations to invite feedback about their leadership style and actions from other staff, including those they supervise.

3. School leaders champion a growth-oriented professional culture schoolwide through the following activities:

   a. Embodying and celebrating the values of their school through their daily words and actions, displays and materials related to the school vision, and community meetings and public events

   b. Devoting time and attention to developing and maintaining systems and structures that support transparent and positive school culture (e.g., establishing staff Crews, coaching and evaluation systems, teacher appreciation traditions)

   c. Modeling and promoting EL Education traditions such as opening readings, team-building activities, and staff and student recognition for achievement and acts of character

4. School leaders foster a school culture in which all staff members embody the school's Habits of Character in their words and actions. Leaders do this through modeling, verbalizing the impact of positive behaviors, and providing regular opportunities for staff to self-assess and reflect upon the adult community's adherence to the norms.

5. Colleagues hold each other accountable to following school norms, and leaders address violations directly and constructively when needed.

6. School leaders expect all staff members to take responsibility for all students, not just the ones they interact with regularly. All staff members hold all students accountable for demonstrating Habits of Character in hallways and common spaces and during school-sponsored events off the school grounds.

C. Demonstrating a Commitment to Diversity, Equity, and Inclusion

1. School leaders demonstrate an explicit commitment to diversity, equity, and inclusion in the following ways:

   a. Embracing diversity of all forms as an asset for learning both in the classroom and the school community

   b. Engaging themselves and others in critical reflection on the ways power and privilege affect their lives and the lives of students and families in their school in relation to class, race, gender, language, and other aspects of background and identity

   c. Establishing structures and systems that ensure high levels of student achievement for all students and narrow the opportunity gap for historically underserved groups

   d. Establishing and maintaining an inclusive and welcoming environment for all students and staff members through public displays, communications, traditions, and other practices

   e. Refuting intolerant statements directed at individuals or groups and helping the learning community to respond appropriately when such statements occur

2. School leaders and all staff members discuss students and their families respectfully and as confidentially as the context requires. Their words and actions demonstrate an asset-based view of students and families, a commitment to inclusion, belief in all students' capacity to succeed, and a consistent problem-solving orientation.

D. Cultivating Emotional Intelligence

1. School leaders demonstrate an accurate awareness of their strengths and limitations and a growth mindset in the pursuit of learning. They believe that with effort, they can succeed in achieving their goals. Their words and actions support all members of the school community to do the same.

2. School leaders productively manage their emotions, including responding to stress, controlling impulses, and engaging in self-discipline and time management in order to complete tasks and pursue personal goals. They manage their responses to disappointment, challenges, and criticism with a mindset that fosters growth. They expect and support others to productively manage their own emotions as well.

3. School leaders are able to consider the varied perspectives of the full range of stakeholders in their school community. They demonstrate reflective listening and empathy by naming and acknowledging these perspectives. They deliberately coach staff members to do the same.

4. School leaders reflect openly on successes and setbacks in order to learn from them productively. They provide structured opportunities and scaffolding for others to do the same.

Core Practice 35
Promoting Shared Leadership

In the EL Education model, leadership is a collaborative, dynamic effort toward a common vision for teaching and learning. Thus, in addition to creating the conditions for all staff to learn, school leaders create the conditions for all staff to lead. Leaders articulate and uphold clear decision-making processes, as well as roles and responsibilities for decisions that impact the learning community. Leaders strategically build the leadership capacity of others; they set up structures for staff and other members of the school community to take responsibility for school improvement efforts and empower these individuals to lead the work. High-functioning, data-informed, impact-oriented teams of educators drive improvement across the school.

Note: "School leaders" in this section refers to district leaders, principals, instructional coaches and guides, and teachers in leadership roles. "Administrative leaders" refers specifically to principals or leaders in district, executive, or supervisory roles.

A. Developing an Instructional Leadership Team

1. Administrative leaders establish an Instructional Leadership Team (ILT) whose charge is to increase the learning and engagement of every student across EL Education's Dimensions of Student Achievement.

2. The ILT includes representatives of multiple stakeholder groups, including administrators, classroom teachers, and specialists. The team is typically limited to 10 or fewer members, providing balanced perspectives and expertise, but not necessarily representing every team or stakeholder group.

3. The ILT meets at least monthly and typically more frequently.

4. The ILT leads an ongoing school improvement process at the macro level, with attention to the five domains of schooling: curriculum, instruction, assessment, culture and character, and leadership. The ILT does not address non-instructional school improvement efforts (e.g., facilities, fund-raising events). The ILT's efforts are deeply aligned to the school's work plan. (See also *Core Practice 33: Leading Evidence-Based Strategic Improvement.*) The ILT's actions include:

   a. Regularly monitoring student achievement across EL Education's Dimensions of Student Achievement

   b. Monitoring progress on school goals and benchmarks

   c. Analyzing data relevant to student achievement, including data about instructional practice, school culture, and family involvement

   d. Identifying grade levels, subgroups, and/or disciplines that need additional support

   e. Adjusting the school work plan to respond to current data by making course corrections (e.g., professional learning, changes to instruction or other programs, improvements in schedules) designed to result in student achievement

   f. Recommending resources to best support student achievement

B. Establishing and Supporting Teams Focused on Impact

1. School leaders facilitate the formation of additional teams as needed, whose work parallels the work of the Instructional Leadership Team at a micro level. These teams analyze specific subsets of data and lead improvement for grade levels, subject areas, or specific subgroups of students (e.g., multitiered system of support teams).

2. Team leaders use evidence of student learning across EL Education's Dimensions of Student Achievement to shape improvement initiatives. Ongoing team practices include:

   a. Collaboratively analyzing data from formative and summative assessments, as well as student work, and discussing the implications for instructional practices, assessment design, and student performance

   b. Analyzing assessment results for individual students, subgroups, and classes

   c. Creating action plans that articulate steps teachers will take to increase student achievement (e.g., improving teaching strategies, re-teaching, tuning the curriculum, implementing academic interventions)

   d. Regularly reassessing and revising action plans based on new data

Promoting Shared Leadership (continued)

C. Building the Capacity of Others to Lead

1. School leaders provide opportunities for faculty to develop leadership through authentic practice (e.g., leading teams, committees, professional learning, whole-school celebrations, family events).

2. School leaders model and coach team leaders to thoughtfully plan and facilitate meetings that maximize the effectiveness of their teams. They encourage the following practices:

   a. Building a strong team culture in which members are invested in collective student achievement and in each others' professional growth

   b. Using tools such as agendas and protocols that foster productive, collaborative inquiry focused on teaching and learning

   c. Prioritizing student learning over adult preferences

   d. Documenting discussion and decisions made during meetings

   e. Holding each other accountable for following group norms and following through on team commitments

3. School leaders provide professional learning focused on leadership skills.

4. School leaders sometimes provide release time or stipends that incentivize teachers to lead.

5. School leaders give those who are learning to lead helpful and specific feedback designed to improve their leadership practice.

D. Supporting Shared Decision-Making

1. School leaders articulate and publicly share the decision-making model that describes the kinds of decisions to be made in any given situation and identifies who is responsible for making each kind of decision. Whenever possible, they empower teachers to take the lead in decisions that directly impact teachers and students.

2. School leaders proactively consult teachers and parents on important school concerns and seek diverse perspectives on issues when they are the sole decision maker.

3. Leaders promote opportunities for discussion and debate about initiatives that impact teaching and learning; following those discussions, staff members uphold the decisions and implement action plans made by school leaders.

4. School leaders establish systems for monitoring and supporting the work of teacher- or family-led teams or committees and for communicating and coordinating the decisions and actions of various teams.

Core Practice 36
Leading Professional Learning

School leaders using the EL Education model respect teachers and other staff members as creative agents in their classrooms and as professionals continually seeking to improve their craft. The EL Education model supports leaders to demonstrate a growth mindset and a commitment to continuous professional learning in themselves and all faculty members. School leaders build capacity in teachers in order to improve student achievement and to sustain teacher commitment, motivation, retention, and performance. Leaders establish and communicate high expectations for learning in the classroom. They conduct classroom learning walks to ask "what's working?" and use evidence from their observations to inform professional learning, formal coaching cycles, and evaluation systems. They conduct regular walk-through observations to assess whether professional learning is being applied effectively and continually improve professional learning systems to impact student achievement.

Note: "School leaders" in this section refers to district leaders, principals, instructional coaches and guides, and teachers in leadership roles. "Administrative leaders" refers specifically to principals or leaders in district, executive, or supervisory roles.

A. Creating a Culture of Adult Learning

1. School leaders model being "lead learners" by engaging in on-site and off-site professional learning to ensure the school's success. They participate fully in professional learning led by other staff members or EL Education coaches.

2. Administrative leaders maximize resource allocation for professional learning, including time, space, salary, and training for instructional coaches and other non-classroom positions that enhance teacher learning and build greater capacity for implementation.

3. School leaders align professional learning with the goals and strategies identified by the instructional leadership team as ones that will lead to increased student achievement.

4. School leaders ensure that all staff members participate in professional learning appropriate to their professional goals and aligned with the school's work plan. They document participation as necessary to fulfill teachers' licensure and certification requirements.

5. Leaders and teachers reflect on, document, and celebrate their learning just as students do.

B. Providing High-Quality Professional Learning

1. School leaders assume primary responsibility for coordinating and, over time, facilitating on-site professional learning aligned with the EL Education model and the school's work plan and student achievement benchmarks. School leaders ensure that professional learning sessions are purposeful, deeply planned, timely, and applicable to faculty who attend.

   a. Professional learning is designed to improve educator practice and increase student achievement while accounting for the characteristics and needs of adult learners.

   b. School leaders model and encourage other facilitators to use EL Education professional learning and facilitation practices so that teachers experience the same kinds of challenging and engaging instruction they will use in their own classrooms.

   c. When appropriate, school leaders differentiate professional learning (e.g., by level of experience, subject area, role, or professional goal) in order to have the greatest impact on teacher practice and student achievement.

2. School leaders create multiple structures to provide consistent and frequent professional learning opportunities. These may include:

   a. On-site, job-embedded professional learning for all staff

   b. Differentiated professional learning sessions

   c. Off-site professional learning

   d. Book studies in which faculty read and discuss a professional text over several sessions

   e. Lesson studies in which faculty co-plan and teach a lesson, observe each other, and revise instruction based on their findings

3. School leaders identify faculty members who demonstrate a high level of success and engagement with the EL Education model. They encourage these individuals to share their expertise with the greater network through modeling, mentoring, presentation at conferences, and other opportunities.

Leading Professional Learning (continued)

C. Providing Frequent Descriptive Feedback

1. Teams of school leaders and teachers regularly conduct learning walks and walk-throughs in order to define and discuss the qualities of effective instruction. To that end:

   a. Learning walks are designed to ask questions (e.g., How are teachers using learning targets in their lessons?) that generate discussion and brainstorming about next steps for teacher learning or school improvement.

   b. Walk-throughs are designed to collect quantitative data on consistencies or quality of instruction across the school. The collected data is used to assess the effectiveness of professional learning and progress on school goals, not to evaluate individual teachers.

   c. Feedback from learning walks and walk-throughs is always aggregated and anonymous; it does not call out individual teachers.

   d. Following learning walks and walk-throughs, school leaders provide timely and specific written feedback describing their findings to the whole staff.

2. Administrative leaders conduct formal observations aligned with required evaluation tools and structures. Whenever possible, formal observations are conducted in a spirit of supportive collaboration toward growth. Observation for the purpose of evaluation is something done with teachers, not to them. (See also *Core Practice 37: Ensuring High-Quality Instruction.*)

3. School leaders supplement formal observations with informal, drop-in mini-observations.

   a. Mini-observations may be set up as lower-stakes visits focused on descriptive feedback as opposed to evaluative feedback.

   b. Mini-observations result in immediate feedback to teachers focused on instructional priorities and school goals.

   c. Leaders provide feedback that addresses strengths, as well as questions and suggestions.

   d. Leaders use mini-observations to identify methods of support and professional learning actions that will lead to individual teacher growth.

D. Coaching Teachers

1. School leaders determine schedules that allow all teachers, whether one-on-one or in small groups, to engage in non-evaluative coaching cycles with instructional coaches and/or EL Education coaches. Sustainable coaching is grounded by schoolwide structures and systems (e.g., peer observations, provision of substitutes to cover classrooms during coaching meetings).

2. School leaders prioritize which teachers receive coaching and determine the length of coaching cycles. They ensure a connection between the school's work plan and teachers' professional goals.

3. School leaders work with coaches to create a coherent system for instructional coaching that includes coaching cycles, documentation structures, and ways to assess the efficacy of coaching.

4. Coaches structure meetings with teachers to foster inquiry, dialogue, and incremental revision of a teacher's practice based on evidence. A coaching cycle typically includes the following elements:

   a. Goal setting that focuses on improving teacher practice and increasing student achievement

   b. Learning observations (sometimes videotaped)

   c. Data collection

   d. Collaborative lesson planning or teaching

   e. Reflection

   f. Revision of classroom practice

   g. Documentation of results supported by evidence

   h. Discussion of next steps, including targeted professional learning

Core Practice 37
Ensuring High-Quality Instruction

In the EL Education model, school leaders support teachers to use curriculum, instruction, and assessment practices that meet high standards for student achievement, including required district and/or state frameworks. School leaders engage teachers in a collaborative process for curriculum mapping that identifies assessments associated with standards-based learning targets. School leaders allocate the resources teachers need to provide the materials, accommodations, interventions, and extensions that ensure all students can and do access the curriculum. After putting adequate plans and resources in place, school leaders carefully and consistently monitor implementation of agreed-upon curriculum, instruction, and assessment through frequent classroom visits and feedback to teachers. Supervision and evaluation structures are designed to support teacher growth and learning while also maintaining high expectations for follow-through and instructional effectiveness.

Note: "School leaders" in this section refers to district leaders, principals, instructional coaches and guides, and teachers in leadership roles. "Administrative leaders" refers specifically to principals or leaders in district, executive, or supervisory roles.

A. Adopting Comprehensive Standards and Challenging Curricula

1. School leaders adopt academic standards based on state standards and college- and career-readiness indicators.

2. School leaders adopt or support teachers to design curricula aligned with standards that challenge, engage, and empower all students. (See also *Core Practice 1: Choosing, Adapting, and Enhancing Curricula.*)

3. School leaders create timelines and transition plans that allow time and provide resources for supportive professional learning when adopting new standards or new curricula.

4. School leaders support teachers in understanding the design of a curriculum in order to ensure readiness to teach it. Support for teachers includes the following:

   a. Assessing teachers' need for professional learning to support understanding and implementation of a new curriculum

   b. Providing professional learning to unpack a new curriculum so that teachers understand its design, purpose, and methodology

   c. Providing time and support for teachers to learn new content or instructional methods

   d. Providing ongoing support, feedback, and collaborative coaching as teachers implement a new curriculum

5. School leaders schedule time and establish a process for creating and annually reviewing curriculum maps, which act as the foundation for all planning, instruction, and assessment. (See also *Core Practice 2: Mapping Knowledge, Skills, and Habits of Character.*)

B. Aligning Curriculum, Instruction, and Assessment

1. School leaders provide dedicated time and guidance, as well as professional learning, for teachers to create instructional plans, including learning expedition overviews, project plans, assessment plans, and daily lessons.

   a. Leaders create schoolwide systems for archiving, revising, and sharing curricular plans.

   b. Leaders facilitate collaborative planning among teachers working on interdisciplinary or multidisciplinary curricula.

   c. Leaders create structures for new teachers to learn how to use the adopted curriculum with support from experienced teachers.

   d. Leaders provide professional learning and planning time for teachers to develop assessments aligned with standards and curriculum maps.

2. School leaders ensure that teachers have access to the instructional materials and resources necessary to implement the curriculum.

3. School leaders review teachers' instructional plans, provide feedback as appropriate, and/or create opportunities for colleagues to review and critique each other's plans for challenge, engagement, and impact.

4. School leaders acquire high-quality assessment tools aligned to required standards and standardized assessments and support teachers in using these tools to monitor student progress.

C. Balancing Support and Accountability

1. School leaders support teachers to challenge, engage, and empower students through deeper instruction. (See also *Core Practice 11: Delivering Effective Lessons.*)

   a. School leaders regularly review learning targets, classroom assessments, student achievement data, and other indicators of practice to assess whether curriculum and instruction is aligned with standards and is increasing student achievement.

   b. School leaders celebrate examples of positive classroom culture, well-designed curricula, and effective lessons and share these examples with others to replicate successful practice.

   c. School leaders frequently visit classrooms to observe teaching and learning in action and provide timely, descriptive feedback to support improvements in classroom culture and instruction.

2. School leaders engage the faculty in coming to agreement about schoolwide consistencies in instructional practice and classroom and schoolwide culture (e.g., posting a do-now to begin lessons, developing classroom norms, using respectful language in hallways). They hold staff accountable for following through on these agreements and also support creativity, innovation, and individual teaching styles.

D. Supervising and Evaluating Staff

1. Administrative leaders establish systems and structures for supervision that support staff to feel safe, valued, and productive as professional educators.

   a. Administrative leaders ensure that teachers know who supervises them and how to ask for clarification of policy, support, or assistance with immediate concerns.

   b. Administrative leaders intentionally seek to build positive relationships with those they supervise through regular one-on-one check-ins, informal communication, and frequent classroom visits.

   c. Administrative leaders consistently and positively collaborate with teachers they supervise to solve problems (e.g., scheduling, substitute coverage, tardiness, illness).

2. Regardless of whether the school uses a district-mandated staff evaluation instrument or one designed by the school, school leaders set goals with teachers, conduct observations, and provide feedback designed to help teachers improve and students to achieve. To the greatest extent possible:

   a. Evaluations are based on multiple observations or a compilation of evidence over the course of the school year.

   b. Staff members engage actively in their own evaluation process through self-assessment, setting goals, and gathering evidence that demonstrates their growth and achievement.

   c. Administrative leaders align their observation, data analysis, and feedback procedures with the evaluation instrument and staff members' professional goals.

   d. Administrative leaders act swiftly and in alignment with school policy to remove a staff member from the school if repeated efforts to address instructional quality concerns do not result in improved performance.

E. Using Data to Inform Supervision and Intervention

1. Administrative leaders meet individually with teachers to discuss evidence collected during informal and formal observations. These conversations are designed to provide a combination of support and accountability that fosters professional growth and meets the needs of students.

2. Administrative leaders and teachers discuss specific students who are not making expected growth in order to identify appropriate interventions or next steps. They work to meet the needs of all students and to ensure equity in the delivery of instruction and support services.

3. Administrative leaders use evidence from observations and dialogue with staff members to identify the best methods of support and to inform plans for professional learning focused on growth.

4. School leaders collaborate with teachers to disaggregate and analyze student achievement data in ways that help identify the factors influencing student performance. Data analysis is solution-oriented and avoids simplistic assumptions about causality.

Index

A

academic courage, iii, 2, 62
accessibility, 2, 3, 12, 62. See also exceptional learners
accommodations, See differentiation
accountability, staff, 84, 86, 88, 92
accountability, student, 25–26, 52. See also self-direction
achievement, See Dimensions of Student Achievement
advanced learners, 26, 45–46. See also differentiation
adventure, promoting, 62–63
arts, 8, 43–44
assessment, 65–77
    aligning with curriculum and instruction, 91–92
    approach to, iv, vii, 65
    boosting achievement with, 72–73
    checking for understanding, 70–71
    communicating student achievement, 74–76
    and continuous improvement, 82, 83
    culture of engagement and achievement, 67
    curriculum maps, 4–5
    delivering effective lessons, 26
    differentiation, 45–46
    English language learners, 47, 48
    and families, 60, 73, 74
    grades, 74
    group projects, 15
    Habits of Character, 14, 55
    Habits of Scholarship, 52, 54, 72
    high-quality work, 28
    interim, 32, 67, 73, 83
    for learning (formative), 5, 67, 72
    of learning (summative), 72
    learning expeditions, 17
    learning targets, 68–69
    on-demand, 5, 26, 83
    performances, 15
    products, 44
    projects, 14–15
    reading, 32
    selecting, 72
    standardized tests, 72, 73, 83
    using data with students, 73
    writing, 35
audience
    arts, 43, 44
    high-quality work, 27, 29
    learning expeditions, 18
    passage presentations, 76
    writing, 33
authenticity
    approach to, vii
    arts, 43
    high-quality work, 27, 28
    learning expeditions, 18
    science, 39
    social studies, 41
    writing, 33, 34

B

background knowledge, 24, 26, 27, 46
bias, 59, 67, 83

C

career readiness, 6–7
case studies
    arts, 43
    courage and adventure, promoting, 62
    designing, 11
    learning expeditions, 11, 16
    reading, 30
    science, 39
    social studies, 41, 42
    wellness, promoting, 9
    writing, 33
celebrations of learning
    approach to, iv
    communicating student achievement, 74, 75
    creating beautiful spaces, 61
    differentiation and inclusion, 46
    engaging family and community, 60
    habits of character, 52, 53, 55
    Habits of Scholarship, 54
    learning expeditions, 17–18
change management, 82–83
character. See also culture and character; Habits of Character
    arts, 44
    aspects of, 54
    continuous improvement, 83
    delivering lessons effectively, 25
    as dimension of student achievement, vii
    global citizenship, 8
    learning targets, 68
    school vision, 80
classroom management, 25–26
classrooms
    creating beautiful spaces, 61
    organization, 25
    print-rich, 32
    school vision, 80
close reading, 30, 31, 39, 41, 42
coaching of teachers, 89, 90, 91
collaboration
    aligning curriculum, assessment and instruction, 91
    approach to, iii, vi
    Crew, 58
    with experts, 12
college readiness, 6–7, 45, 57, 58
communication
    approach to, vii
    with family, 59–60, 75
    learning targets, 68, 74
    professional culture, cultivating, 85
    school vision, 80
    student achievement, 74–76
community
    communicating student achievement, 75

engaging families and, 59–60
of learning, 52–53
school vision, 80
conferences, student-led
approach to, iv
communicating student achievement, 74, 75
delivering lessons effectively, 26
engaging family, 60
reading, 32
conflicts and conflict resolution
community of learning, 53
courage and adventure, promoting, 63
Crew, 57, 58
family, 59
habits of character, 55
continuous improvement
evidence-based strategic improvement, 82–84
importance of, iv, 79
Instructional Leadership Team, 87
professional culture, cultivating, 85
professional learning, 89
Conversation Cues, 48, 70
core practices. See also assessment; culture and character; curriculum; instruction; leadership
defined, iv
EL approach, v
lists by domain, 1, 21, 51, 65, 79
counselors, 6, 7, 45
courage
academic, iii, 2, 62
mathematical, 36, 37
promoting, 62–63
craftsmanship
college readiness, 7
delivering lessons effectively, 25
high-quality work, vii, 27
learning expeditions, 18
project assessment, 14
writing, 34
Crew
building culture and structure of, 56–58
college readiness support, 6, 7
communicating student achievement, 75, 76
courage and adventure, promoting, 62, 63
culture and character, iv, 51
defined, 56
delivering lessons effectively, 26
English language learners, 48
global citizenship, 8
Habits of Scholarship, 54–55
reading, 32
safety, 9
school vision, 81
wellness, promoting, 9–10
critical thinking, vii, 25
critiques
arts, 43, 44
culture of engagement and achievement, 67
high-quality work, vii, 28
learning expeditions, 16
mathematics, 36, 37
product and performance planning, 15
writing, 33, 34
culminating events, 16, 17–18, 81
culture and character, 51–63
approach to, iv, 51

arts culture, 44
community of learning, 52–53
courage and adventure, promoting, 62–63
creating beautiful spaces, 61
Crew culture and practice, 56–58
curriculum selection, 2
differentiation, 46
engagement and achievement, cultivating, 67
engaging families and the community, 59–60
English language learners, 47, 48
excellence, culture of, 28
global citizenship, supporting, 8
habits of character, fostering, 54–55
learning expeditions, 17
mathematical literacy, culture of, 37–38
professional culture, 85–86, 89
reading, culture of, 31–32
school vision, 80
science inquiry, culture of, 40
writing, 33, 34–35
curriculum, 1–18. See also curriculum maps
aligning with assessment and instruction, 91–92
approach to, iv, vii, 1
archiving, 91
arts, 43
case studies, 11
choosing, adapting, and enhancing, 2–3, 9
college and career readiness, 6–7
Crew, 56, 57
global citizenship, 2, 8
habits of character, fostering, 2, 4–5, 55
incorporating fieldwork, experts, and service learning, 12–13
leadership support, 91
learning expeditions, 16–18
mathematics, 36
projects and products, 14–15
school vision, 80, 81
wellness, promoting, 9–10
curriculum maps
arts, 43
global citizenship, 8
leadership and, 91
learning targets, 68
using, 4–5

D

data collection and analysis
approach to, vii
continuous improvement, 82–84
curriculum selection, 2
equity, 83
Instructional Leadership Team, 87
professional learning, 84, 90
science, 40
social studies, 41, 42
supervising and evaluating staff, 90, 92
using assessment data with students, 73
debriefing
checking for understanding, 71
courage and adventure, promoting, 62
Crew, 57, 58
delivering lessons effectively, 26
high-quality work, 28
learning targets, 69
mathematics, 38

science, 40
    social studies, 42
    Workshop 1.0 lesson format, 23
    writing, 35
design principles, EL, v, vi, 52
differentiation
    arts, 44
    college readiness support, 6
    core practice, 45–46
    curriculum selection and adaptation, 2, 3
    defined, 45
    high-quality work, 27
    IEPs, 45, 46
    importance of, 21, 45
    lesson planning and delivery, 22, 26
    product and performance planning, 15
    reading, 30, 31, 46
    writing, 34
Dimensions of Student Achievement
    achievement, defined, 2
    college readiness support, 7
    communicating achievement, 75
    continuous improvement, 82, 83
    creating beautiful spaces, 61
    importance of, v, vii
    and leadership, iv, 79, 87
    school vision, 80
discipline, 52, 53, 83. See also conflicts and conflict resolution
discovery-based lesson format, 23, 69
displays
    approach to, iii
    arts, 43, 44
    creating beautiful spaces, 61
    learning expeditions, 18
diversity. See also inclusion
    courage and adventure, promoting, 62
    design principle, vi
    differentiation, 46
    English language learners, 47, 48
    global citizenship, 8
    habits of character, fostering, 55
    learning expeditions, 17
    modeling by teachers and leaders, 46
    professional culture, cultivating, 86
    school vision, 80, 81

E

El Education (EL). See also core practices
    approach, iii
    design principles, v, vi, 52
    Implementation Review, 83
emotions, See social and emotional learning
engagement, See participation and engagement
English language learners, 3, 8, 47–48
environmental literacy, 40
environmental stewardship, 2, 8, 17, 40. See also natural world
equity
    approach to, iii
    classroom management, 25
    community of learning, 53
    continuous improvement, 83
    Crew, 56
    curriculum selection, 2
    global citizenship, 8
    habits of character, fostering, 55

    learning expeditions, 17
    modeling by teachers and leaders, 46
    professional culture, cultivating, 86
    social studies, 42
ethics
    approach to, vii
    college readiness support, 6
    community of learning, 52
    curriculum maps, 4
    Habits of Scholarship, 54–55
    service learning, 13
exceptional learners, 3, 6, 45, 81. See also advanced learners; differentiation
expeditions, learning, See learning expeditions
experts
    arts, 43, 44
    culture of engagement and achievement, 67
    engaging community, 60
    feedback from, 28
    high-quality work, 27, 28
    incorporating, 12–13
    learning expeditions, 16
    school vision, 81
    science, 39
    social studies, 41
extracurricular activities, 7, 9, 55, 63

F

family. See also conferences, student-led
    and assessment, 60, 73, 74
    communicating student achievement, 75
    continuous improvement, 83, 84
    Crew, 58
    differentiation, 45, 46
    engaging family and community, 59–60
    English language learners, 47, 48
    handbook, 75, 80
    leadership, promoting shared, 88
    as partners, 59
    school vision, 80, 81
    visits, 59, 81
feedback
    aligning curriculum, assessment and instruction, 91
    arts, 44
    checking for understanding, 70
    continuous improvement, 82
    culture of engagement and achievement, 67
    English language learners, 48
    experts, 28
    family, 59–60
    high-quality work, 28
    leadership, promoting shared, 88
    learning expeditions, 18
    professional learning and culture, 85, 90
    teacher evaluation, 92
    teachers' modeling of, 28
    wellness, promoting, 10
    writing, 34
field trips, 12. See also fieldwork
fieldwork
    arts, 44
    courage and adventure, promoting, 62
    defined, 12
    Habits of Scholarship, 55
    incorporating, 12–13

learning expeditions, 16, 17
safety, 12, 63
school vision, 81
science, 39
social studies, 41
financial aid, 6, 7, 58
formative assessments, 5, 67, 72
Four Ts, 17

G

global citizenship, 2, 8, 55
goals
    checking for understanding, 70–71
    coaching cycles, 90
    communicating student achievement, 74
    continuous improvement, 82
    courage and adventure, promoting, 62
    evaluating staff, 92
    Instructional Leadership Team, 87
    mathematics, 37
    professional learning, 89, 90
    reading, 32
    using assessment data with, 73
grades and grading, 74. See also assessment
graduation celebrations, 7
groups and grouping
    arts, 44
    assessment, 15
    checking for understanding, 70
    delivering lessons effectively, 25
    differentiation, 45, 46
    English language learners, 47
    school vision, 81
growth mindset, 53, 67, 85

H

Habits of Character. See also character; culture and character
    assessment, 14, 55
    checking for understanding, 71
    college readiness support, 6
    communicating student achievement, 75
    community of learning, 52, 53
    continuous improvement, 83
    courage and adventure, promoting, 62–63
    Crew, 57, 58
    curriculum, 2, 4–5, 55
    fostering, 54–55
    global citizenship, 8
    lesson planning, 22
    product and performance planning, 15
    professional culture, cultivating, 86
    reading, 31
Habits of Scholarship/work
    approach to, vii
    assessment, 52, 54, 72
    college readiness support, 6
    communicating student achievement, 74
    community of learning, 52
    continuous improvement, 83
    Crew, 58
    culture of engagement and achievement, 67
    fostering, 54–55
    writing, 34
Hahn, Kurt, 56

health, promoting wellness, 9–10
high-quality work
    approach to, vii
    college readiness support, 6
    continuous improvement, 83
    creating beautiful spaces, 61
    curriculum maps, 5
    differentiation, 46
    learning expeditions, 17
    lesson planning, 22
    planning and supporting, 27–29
    product and performance planning, 15
    school vision, 80
    social studies, 42
    writing, 33, 34

I

IEP (Individualized Education Program), 45, 46
ILT (Instructional Leadership Team), 87
improvement, See continuous improvement
inclusion. See also diversity
    celebrations, 46
    community of learning, 53
    courage and adventure, promoting, 62
    Crew, 56
    English language learners, 48
    global citizenship, 8
    habits of character, fostering, 55
    professional culture, cultivating, 86
Individualized Education Program (IEP), 45, 46
instruction, 21–49
    aligning with assessment and curriculum, 91–92
    approach to, iv, vii, 21
    arts, 43–44
    checking for understanding, 70–71
    delivering effective lessons, 25–26
    differentiating core practice, 45–46
    English language learners, 3, 8, 47–48
    habits of character, fostering, 54–55
    high-quality, ensuring, 91–92
    high-quality work, 27–29
    lesson planning, 22–24
    mathematics, 36–38
    reading, 30–32
    school vision, 80
    science, 39–40
    social studies, 41–42
    writing, 33–35
Instructional Leadership Team (ILT), 87
interim assessment, 32, 67, 73, 83
internships, 6, 56

J

justice, restorative, 52, 57, 58
justice, social, See social justice

K

kickoff experiences, 16, 17–18

L

labs, 37, 39
Language Dives, 48

language learning, 3, 8, 47–48
leadership, 79–92. See also leadership, student
    approach to, iv, vii, 79
    Crew, 57
    development, 88
    ensuring high-quality instruction, 91–92
    professional culture, cultivating, 85–86
    professional learning, promoting, 89–90, 91
    school vision, fostering, 80–81
    shared leadership, promoting, iv, 79, 87–88
    strategic improvement, 82–84
    supporting and evaluating staff, 92
leadership, shared, iv, 79, 87–88
leadership, student
    approach to, vii
    community of learning, 52, 53
    courage and adventure, promoting, 62
    learning expeditions, 16
    lesson planning, 22
learning, approach to, iii
learning disabilities, See students with disabilities
learning expeditions
    arts, 43
    case studies, 11, 16
    continuous improvement, 83
    courage and adventure, promoting, 62
    curriculum maps, 4
    designing, 16–18
    reading, 30
    social studies, 41
    wellness, promoting, 9
    writing, 33
learning targets
    checking for understanding, 70
    communicating student achievement, 74
    crafting and using, 68–69
    Crew, 57
    culture of engagement and achievement, 67
    curriculum maps, 4–5
    delivering lessons effectively, 25
    differentiation, 46
    English language learners, 47
    learning expeditions, 17
    mathematics, 36, 37
    project design, 14
    review by leaders, 92
    science, 39
    writing, 33
learning walks, 89, 90
lessons
    delivering effective, 25–26
    formats, 22, 23–24, 30
    planning effective, 22–24
literacy
    curriculum maps, 5
    environmental, 40
    high-quality work, 27
    learning expeditions, 16
    mathematical, 37–38
    project design, 14
    reading core practice, 30–32
    technological, 6–7

M

maps, curriculum, See curriculum maps
mastery of knowledge and skills dimension of achievement, vii
mathematics
    assessment, 36, 38
    case studies, 11
    courage, 36, 37
    learning expeditions, 16
    project design, 14
    teaching core practice, 36–38
meetings
    Crew, 57
    leadership, 81, 85
    staff, 81
mental health, 9–10
mini-observations, 90
modeling by teachers and leaders
    approach to, vii
    commitment to equity and diversity, 46
    community of learning, 52
    continuous improvement, 84
    courage and adventure, promoting, 62
    Crew, 56
    feedback, 28
    habits of character, 52, 54, 55
    leadership, 88
    mathematics, 36, 37–38
    professional culture and learning, 85, 89
    reading, 31–32
    wellness, promoting, 9
    writing, 34

N

natural world
    courage and adventure, promoting, 62
    creating beautiful spaces, 61
    environmental stewardship, 2, 8, 17, 40
    global citizenship, 8
    science, 39, 40
    wellness, promoting, 9
norms
    community of learning, 53
    continuous improvement, 84
    courage and adventure, promoting, 63
    ethics, 54
    Habits of Character, 52, 55
    high-quality work, 28
    mathematics, 37
    professional culture, cultivating, 85, 86

O

observation
    checking for understanding, 70
    continuous improvement, 83
    evaluating staff, 92
    learning walks, 89, 90
    mathematics, 38
    mini-observations, 90
    professional learning, 89, 90
    reading, 32
    walk-throughs, 90
on-demand assessment, 5, 26, 83
outdoor spaces and experiences, 9, 40, 61, 62
Outward Bound, 56, 62

P

participation and engagement
    approach to, vii
    checking for understanding, 70
    continuous improvement, 83
    culture of engagement and achievement, 67
    differentiation, 46
    family and community, 46, 59–60
    lesson delivery and format, 23, 25
    professional learning, 89
passage presentations, iv, 74, 75–76
peer critiques and feedback, 34, 70
peer teaching, 40
performances
    arts, teaching, 43, 44
    continuous improvement, 83
    curriculum maps, 5
    designing and planning, 14–15
perseverance. See also Habits of Character
    approach to, vi, vii
    arts, teaching, 44
    culture of engagement and achievement, 67
physical education, 9, 10
portfolios
    art, 44
    communicating student achievement, 74, 75, 76
    and Crew, 57, 58
    mathematics, 38
    writing, 35
problem solving, 37, 41, 55, 59
products
    assessment, 44
    continuous improvement, 83
    designing and planning, 14–15
    Habits of Character, fostering, 55
    high-quality work, 27
    school vision, 81
professional culture, cultivating, 85–86
professional learning (professional development)
    assessment, 73
    community of learning, 53
    continuous improvement, 82–83, 84
    courage and adventure, promoting, 63
    Crew, building culture of, 56
    data, 84, 90
    differentiation, 45
    English language learners, 47
    growth mindset, 67, 85
    leadership, promoting shared, 88
    leadership, role in, 89–90, 91
    opportunities for, 89
    school vision, 81
progress reports, 74
projects
    arts, 43
    designing, 14–15
    learning expeditions, 16
    reading, 30
    science, 39
    social studies, 41
    writing, 33
protocols
    checking for understanding, 70
    continuous improvement, 83, 84
    courage and adventure, promoting, 63
    Crew, building culture of, 56

    delivering lessons effectively, 25–26
    English language learners, 48
    high-quality work, 28
    leadership, promoting shared, 88
    mathematics, 37
    professional culture, cultivating, 85
    protocol-based lesson format, 23–24
    reading, 30, 31
    school vision, 81

Q

quality, See high-quality work
quick-check techniques, 70

R

reading
    close, 30, 31, 39, 41, 42
    culture of, 31–32
    differentiation, 30, 31, 46
    teaching core practice, 30–32
reflection
    approach to, iii, vi
    checking for understanding, 70–71
    coaching cycles, 90
    courage and adventure, promoting, 62, 63
    Crew, 57, 58
    culture of engagement and achievement, 67
    delivering lessons effectively, 26
    high-quality work, 28
    professional learning, 89, 90
report cards, 74–75
restorative justice, 52, 57, 58
revision
    approach to, vii
    arts, 43, 44
    high-quality work, 29
    learning expeditions, 16
    writing, 33, 34
risk-taking
    arts, 43
    courage and adventure, promoting, 62
    English language learners, 48
    mathematics, 36, 37
    professional culture, cultivating, 85
    reading, 31
    writing, 34
rubrics
    arts, 44
    assessment data, 83
    communicating student achievement, 74, 75–76
    culture of engagement and achievement, 67
    Habits of Scholarship, 54
    high-quality work, 27, 28, 29
    projects and products, 14, 15
    writing, 33, 34, 35

S

safety
    community of learning, 52
    courage and adventure, promoting, 62–63
    Crew, 9
    fieldwork, 12, 63
    high-quality work, 28
    wellness, promoting, 9

Scholarship, Habits of, See Habits of Scholarship/work
school vision, 80–81, 82
science, teaching core practice, 39–40
self-assessment
    arts, 44
    boosting student achievement, 72
    checking for understanding, 70–71
    Crew, 56
    culture of engagement and achievement, 67
    delivering lessons effectively, 26
    English language learners, 47
    Habits of Character, 55
    high-quality work, 28
    by staff, 86, 92
    writing, 35
self-direction
    approach to, iv, vi
    arts, 44
    community of learning, 53
    high-quality work, 28
    project design, 14
service and service learning
    approach to, vi, vii
    communicating student achievement, 75
    core practice, 12–13
    curriculum selection, 2
    Habits of Character, fostering, 55
    high-quality work, 28
    learning expeditions, 16
    social studies, 42
shared leadership, iv, 79, 87–88
social and emotional learning
    approach to, vii
    courage and adventure, promoting, 63
    professional culture, cultivating, 86
    wellness, promoting, 9–10
social justice
    approach to, iii
    curriculum selection, 2
    global citizenship, 8
    Habits of Character, fostering, 55
    learning expeditions, 17
    service learning, 13
social studies, teaching core practice, 41–42
sports and sportsmanship, 9, 62–63
standardized tests, 72, 73, 83
standards
    arts, 43
    assessment selection, 72
    communicating student achievement, 74
    culture of engagement and achievement, 67
    curriculum maps, 4–5
    curriculum selection, 2
    high-quality work, 28
    learning expeditions, 16–17
    learning targets, 67, 68
    lesson planning, 22
    mathematics, 36
    reading, 31
    science, 39
    social studies, 41
strategic improvement, 82–84. See also continuous improvement
student-engaged assessment, See assessment; self-assessment
student leadership, See leadership, student
students with disabilities. See also differentiation
    college readiness support, 6

    courage and adventure, promoting, 62
    curriculum selection and adaption, 2, 3
    fieldwork, 12
summative assessment, 72
supplementary services, 45, 47

T

targets, learning, See learning targets
teachers and staff. See also professional learning
    accountability, 84, 86, 88, 92
    continuous improvement, 82
    Crew, culture of, 56
    Dimensions of Student Achievement, vii
    English language learners, 48
    evaluating, 92
    leadership, promoting shared, 87–88
    professional culture, cultivating, 85–86
    roles and responsibilities, 82
    school vision, 80–81
    using data, 84
teamwork, See Crew
technology
    college readiness support, 6–7
    continuous improvement, 83
    curriculum selection, 2
    engaging with families and community, 60, 80
    literacy, 6–7
    mathematics, 36, 37
    products and performance planning, 15
topic selection for learning expeditions, 16–17
tracking, 81
transcripts, 74–75
transitions, 91
trust
    approach to, iv, vi
    delivering lessons effectively, 26
    engaging with families and community, 59
    leadership, iv, 79, 85
    professional culture, cultivating, 85

U

understanding, checking for, 70–71

V

vision, school, 80–81, 82
visitors and guests, 7, 59, 81, 92
volunteers, 59, 60

W

walk-throughs, 90
wellness, promoting, 9–10
work, See high-quality work
work, habits of, See Habits of Scholarship/work
Workshop 1.0 and 2.0 lesson formats, 23, 69, 70
writing
    culture of, 34–35
    in Dimensions of Student Achievement, vii
    science, 40
    social studies, 42
    teaching core practice, 33–35

www.ingramcontent.com/pod-product-compliance
Lightning Source LLC
Chambersburg PA
CBHW081936110426
42742CB00040BA/3276